TURNKEY REAL ESTATE INVESTING

OVERCOME ANALYSIS PARALYSIS: PROVEN STRATEGIES TO SIDESTEP COSTLY MISTAKES AND BUY YOUR FIRST RENTAL PROPERTY TO ESTABLISH CONSISTENT MONTHLY CASH FLOW

CHRISTOPHER A. STEVENS

CONTENTS

INTRODUCTION

Let me take you back to when I made my first real estate investment. Picture a young, eager investor who knew almost nothing about the game. I was excited but also terrified. I had a bit of capital saved up and felt ready to make my move. One day while I was working my day job, I stumbled upon a modest condo in Las Vegas that seemed perfect. It was 2011 when the real estate market was in turmoil. The numbers looked good, but doubts started to creep in. What if there were repairs I couldn't afford? What if I couldn't find tenants? What if I was making a huge mistake?

These questions swirled in my head, paralyzing me with fear. I spent countless nights researching, analyzing, and second-guessing myself. But then, I realized something crucial: I was never going to have all the answers. I had to take that leap of faith. So, I did. I bought the property, and guess what? It turned out to be one of the best decisions of my life. That condo not only provided a steady income but also became the foundation for my future investments. It wasn't always smooth sailing, but each challenge taught me something invaluable.

The other thing I learned was to buy and hold when you're able. I sold the Las Vegas property and doubled my investment in about two years. I needed the funds for another real estate investment. Had I been able to keep the Las Vegas property, that property would have averaged an annual 22% gain. To put that into perspective, it's been 13 years since I purchased the Las Vegas property. With a 22% annual gain for 13 years, the total ROI would be approximately 906.2%. So, a $25,000 investment would turn into $226,500 after 13 years.

Analysis Paralysis: It's a problem many potential investors face. You have enough knowledge to know the risks and the rewards, but that same knowledge keeps you stuck in a loop of indecision. This book aims to break that cycle. I'm here to provide actionable steps and practical advice to help you overcome your fears and make your first (or next) real estate investment.

Who am I to give you this advice? I'm someone who has been in your shoes. With over two decades of experience in real estate investing, I've seen a lot. I'm still learning, but I now own six properties—one I self-manage and five that are handled by property managers. My journey has been filled with ups and downs, but each experience has made me wiser and more equipped to guide you.

The primary goal of this book is simple: to help you purchase your first single-family real estate investment by overcoming analysis paralysis. We'll walk through the entire process together, step by step. From understanding market trends to securing financing, and from managing properties to ethical investing. This book covers it all.

Who is this book for? This book is for every kind of investor looking to get started in residential real estate investing. You need some capital to invest (25-30% down payment and at least six months of payments for reserves), and a basic understanding of real estate. Most likely, you have a lot of knowledge and have been considering real estate investing for many years, but something is holding you back. Whether it's fear, uncertainty, or just plain indecision—this book is designed to help you get past that.

Who is this book not for? This book is NOT for those who have zero capital. There are many books about how to get into real estate investing with "no money down." For 99.9% of the population, that's not realistic. You must have some money saved towards a down payment of about 25-30%. Plus, you always need to have some reserves to weather any other challenges or bumps in the road. Bumps WILL happen but don't fret. Stick with it, and in the long run, you'll see big gains.

Turnkey residential single-family properties are a fantastic starting point for beginners. Why? They're ready to rent out immediately, which means less hassle and quicker returns. You don't have to worry about renovations or repairs. You can start earning income in about one month. This book will show you why turnkey properties are ideal for your first investment and how to find the right one for you.

Let's talk Structure: The book is organized into easy-to-follow chapters.

- We'll start with understanding your financial standing and setting investment goals.
- Next, we'll dive into market analysis and property selection.
- Then, we'll cover financing options and the buying process.
- We'll also discuss property management—whether you choose to do it yourself or hire a manager.
- Finally, we'll touch on ethical investing—*because doing the right thing while doing well is important.*

What can you expect to gain from this book? Practical tools, real-life examples, and actionable insights. At the end, you'll find an Action Item List and tips from my own experiences. When you finish this book, you'll have the confidence and knowledge to make your first real estate investment.

So, are you ready to take the plunge? It's time to turn your dreams into reality. This book will guide you every step of the way, ensuring that your first investment is a successful one. Let's get started on this exciting journey together. Adventure awaits.

Important Notice: This book does NOT provide financial advice. I am NOT an investment advisor. I do qualify, under the United States tax code, as a **Real Estate Professional**. My credentials are my own experiences that have helped me get to the level of an Accredited Investor (not based on income, but on net worth). My latest Accreditation Verification Letter is from Parallel Markets, dated October 30, 2024. For more information on Accredited Investors visit: https://www.investopedia.com/terms/a/accreditedinvestor.asp.

The information in this book is intended for general education only and is **not specific investment advice**. You are ultimately responsible for your investment decisions; this is only a guide to help provide information. The investments you make could lead to significant financial losses, depending on your decisions. Past results are no guarantee of future performance.

1

OVERCOMING ANALYSIS PARALYSIS

You ever had that moment when you're staring at a menu, and everything looks so good that you just can't decide? You end up ordering the same old burger because it's safe, even though you really wanted to try that new spicy chicken sandwich? That's analysis paralysis in a nutshell. Now, imagine that menu is filled with real estate opportunities and your indecision is costing you potential wealth. Scary, right?

Let's be honest, getting started in real estate can be overwhelming. You have some capital, you know a bit about the market, but the idea of making that first investment is terrifying – you might even say "paralyzing." What if you mess up? What if you pick the wrong property or the market crashes? These thoughts swirl around in your head, leaving you stuck—paralyzed by analysis. I get it. I've been there. The good news is you're not alone, and this chapter will help you break free from this mental gridlock.

UNDERSTANDING ANALYSIS PARALYSIS IN REAL ESTATE

Analysis paralysis is a psychological phenomenon where overthinking and overanalyzing data prevent you from making a decision. It's like having too many tabs open in your brain's browser, and none of them are loading. This paralysis is especially prevalent in real estate investing. The stakes are high, and the fear of making a costly mistake can be paralyzing.

One of the biggest psychological barriers is the fear of making mistakes. You've got some capital, and the last thing you want is to see it disappear because of a bad investment. This fear often leads to overanalyzing every detail to the point where you can't decide. You start thinking about every possible scenario, every potential pitfall, and before you know it, months have passed, and you're still sitting on the sidelines.

Another issue is the sheer volume of information available. You dive into market trends, property values, financing options, and legalities. It's like drinking from a firehose. The more information you consume, the more overwhelmed you get. This overload can lead to constant second-guessing, where you're always seeking more data to validate your thoughts. You convince yourself that just one more article, one more podcast, will give you the clarity you need. Spoiler alert: it won't.

The symptoms of analysis paralysis are easy to spot once you know what to look for. Frequent second-guessing is a big one. You find yourself revisiting the same properties, re-running the numbers, and still not feeling confident enough to pull the trigger. Constantly seeking more information is another sign. If you're always in research mode but never in action mode, you're likely stuck in analysis paralysis. The inability to make decisions is the final nail in the coffin. You have all the information you need, but you just can't bring yourself to make a move.

Not overcoming analysis paralysis can have serious consequences:

- ✓ You end up *missing out* on investment opportunities that could have been profitable. The real estate market doesn't wait for you to make up your mind. Good deals come and go, and if you're always in analysis mode, you'll watch them slip away.
- ✓ *Financial stagnation* is another risk. Without taking action, your capital just sits there, not growing, not working for you.
- ✓ This inaction can also lead to *increased stress and anxiety*. You're constantly thinking about what could have been, which adds to the pressure and makes it even harder to make decisions in the future.

But enough about the doom and gloom. Let's talk about overcoming analysis paralysis.

Scenario 1: Take John, for example. John was a first-time investor who spent months analyzing properties, crunching numbers, and reading every real estate book he could find. He was stuck. Then, he decided to take a leap of faith. He bought a modest single-family home in a growing neighborhood. Yes, he was scared, but he trusted his research and took the plunge. Today, that property is generating steady rental income, and John has since acquired two more properties. What changed? He learned to trust his gut and take calculated risks.

Don't just take it from me. Successful investors often share similar stories. They've been where you are—stuck in analysis paralysis—but they took action and learned from their experiences. One investor I spoke with said, "The first deal is always the hardest. Once you get over that initial fear, each subsequent deal becomes easier." Another investor mentioned how they used real estate investment software to streamline their decision-making process. Tools like *Mashvisor* helped them quickly analyze properties and make informed decisions without getting bogged down by data.

Overcoming analysis paralysis is about taking that first step. It's about trusting your research, accepting that no deal is perfect, and understanding that every investment carries some level of risk. The key is to act on good deals rather than waiting for the perfect one that may never come. So, let's break free from the chains of indecision and start making moves. Your future self will thank you.

SETTING CLEAR INVESTMENT GOALS

Imagine setting out on a road trip without a map or GPS. You might have a general idea of where you want to go, but without clear directions, you'll probably end up lost. The same principle applies to real estate investing. Setting specific, measurable, and time-bound goals is like plotting your route and setting your destination. It gives you a clear path to follow and milestones to celebrate along the way. Goals are crucial for overcoming analysis paralysis because they provide focus and direction, reducing the overwhelming feeling of not knowing where to start.

One effective framework for setting goals is the SMART goals framework, which stands for Specific, Measurable, Attainable, Relevant, and Time-based. By setting SMART goals, you ensure that your objectives are clear and achievable. Specific goals answer the questions of who, what, where, when, and why. Measurable goals allow you to track your progress and know when you've achieved them. Attainable goals are realistic and achievable, given your current resources and constraints. Relevant goals align with your broader objectives and values. Time-based goals have a clear deadline, creating a sense of urgency and focus.

When setting investment goals, it's important to balance long-term and short-term objectives. Long-term goals might include owning a certain number of properties in ten years or generating a specific amount of passive income. Short-term goals could be more immediate, like saving for a down payment within six months or attending a real estate workshop next month. Both types of goals are essential. Long-term goals provide a vision for the future, while short-term goals offer immediate steps to get there.

Let's walk through the process of setting your own investment goals. Start by identifying your financial targets. Ask yourself how much money you want to make from your real estate investments. Be specific. Are you aiming for a monthly cash flow of $200? Or perhaps you want to increase your net worth by $100,000 in five years? Once you have a clear financial target, determine the types of properties you're interested in. For this book, we'll focus on turnkey single-family homes, but eventually you can focus on fixer-uppers, multi-family units, or perhaps commercial properties. Knowing your preferred property type helps narrow your options and focus your research.

Next, set your investment timeline. Break down your long-term goals into smaller, manageable steps. For instance, if your long-term goal is to own five properties in ten years, your short-term goal might be to purchase your first property within the next six months. Setting a timeline creates a sense of urgency and helps you stay on track.

While setting goals, it's important to avoid common pitfalls. One major mistake is setting unrealistic expectations. It's easy to get carried away with ambitious goals, but setting the bar too high can lead to frustration and burnout. Be honest with yourself about what's achievable given your current resources and constraints. Another pitfall is a lack of flexibility. Life happens, and sometimes things don't go as planned. Be prepared to adjust your goals as needed. Flexibility doesn't mean abandoning your goals; it means adapting to changing circumstances while staying focused on your broader objectives.

To track and measure your progress, use practical tools. Investment tracking spreadsheets are a great way to organize your goals and monitor your progress. You can create a simple spreadsheet to track key metrics like cash flow, property values, and expenses. There are also real estate investment apps that offer robust tracking and analysis features.

Apps like *Stessa* and *Property Buddy* can help you keep tabs on your investments, provide insights, and even generate reports. These tools make it easier to see how far you've come and what steps you need to take next.

Remember the analogy of the road trip? Think of these tools as your GPS. They help you stay on course and make adjustments as needed. By setting clear goals and regularly tracking your progress, you'll find it easier to overcome analysis paralysis and take decisive action. You'll have a clear sense of direction, know what you're working towards, and be able to celebrate your achievements along the way.

BUILDING CONFIDENCE THROUGH EDUCATION

Education is your secret weapon in real estate investing. Think of it like this: you wouldn't jump out of a plane without a parachute, so why dive into real estate without arming yourself with knowledge? Continuous learning helps you mitigate fear and build confidence. The more you know, the less daunting those investment decisions become. Attending **real estate workshops** can be a game-changer. These events provide valuable insights from seasoned pros, and they offer a chance to ask questions and get immediate answers. Plus, you'll meet other investors who are in the same boat, which can be incredibly reassuring.

Reading **industry publications** is another way to stay sharp. Journals, magazines, and online articles keep you updated on market trends, legal changes, and new investment strategies. They're like your daily vitamins—keeping you healthy and informed. But let's not stop there. **Books, podcasts, and**

online courses are fantastic resources. If you haven't read *Rich Dad Poor Dad* by Robert Kiyosaki, make it your next read. This book breaks down financial literacy in a way that's easy to understand and incredibly motivating. It's a staple for anyone looking to build wealth through real estate.

Podcasts are another goldmine: My #1 **favorite podcast** about all kinds of investing is the **The Money Ripples Podcast**. The Money Ripples Podcast isn't just about real estate investing, so keep that in mind. However, the week before publishing this book, Chris Miles (the host) released a podcast about *How to Overcome Your Fear of Investing*. The timing couldn't have been better, and the message will help you.

Give this podcast a listen: https://www.youtube.com/watch?v=RbAdbSrrdgE

More specifically about real estate, The *BiggerPockets* Real Estate Podcast, is packed with interviews from successful investors, offering practical advice and inspiring stories. You can listen during your commute, workout, or even while cooking dinner. It's like having a mentor in your ear, guiding you through the complexities of real estate investing. Online courses can also be invaluable. Websites like *Coursera* and *Udemy* offer courses on everything from real estate finance to property management. These courses allow you to learn at your own pace, making them perfect for fitting into a busy schedule.

Now, let's break down some key **concepts** and **terminology** you'll encounter in your real estate journey. Understanding these terms will not only boost your confidence but also ensure you're speaking the same language as other investors.

✓ First up is **cash flow**.

- ○ This is the net income you receive from a property after all expenses are paid. Think of it as your property's paycheck. Positive cash flow means your investment is making money, while negative cash flow indicates a loss.

✓ Next, we have the **cap rate**, or **capitalization rate**. This metric helps you evaluate the return on an investment property.

- ○ It's calculated by dividing the property's net operating income by its current market value. A higher cap rate typically suggests a better return, but it's essential to consider the risks associated with those higher returns.

✓ **Leverage** is another crucial term. In real estate, leverage refers to using borrowed capital to increase the potential return on investment. Essentially, it's using other people's money to grow your wealth. While leverage can amplify gains, it can also magnify losses, so it's important to use it wisely.

✓ **Networking** with experienced investors is another powerful way to build confidence.

- ○ Real estate investment clubs are fantastic places to meet like-minded individuals. These clubs often host meetings, workshops, and social events where you can learn from others' experiences and share your own. Online forums and communities, like *BiggerPockets*, are also great for networking. You can ask questions, share insights, and even find potential partners for investment deals. It's like having a support group that's always available, no matter where you are.

✓ **Learning from peers and mentors** can provide invaluable insights. They've been through all of the ups and downs and can offer advice that you won't find in books or articles.

○ Don't be afraid to reach out and ask questions. Most seasoned investors are happy to share their knowledge and help newcomers succeed. Remember, confidence comes from knowledge and experience. The more you learn, the more empowered you'll feel to make informed decisions. So, embrace continuous learning, and watch your confidence—and your wealth—grow.

CREATING AN ACTIONABLE INVESTMENT PLAN

Creating an actionable investment plan is like plotting your course before setting sail. You wouldn't head out into open waters without a map, right? The same logic applies here. A detailed investment plan helps you navigate the complexities of real estate investing, ensuring you stay on course and reach your destination.

First, let's talk about defining your investment criteria. This is your compass. You need to know what kind of properties you're looking for and what your financial parameters are. To keep it simple, we'll focus on turnkey single-family homes. Next, what's your budget? What's your desired location? With turnkey properties, you're a bit more limited on locations, but you'll have some choices. Answering these questions helps narrow your focus and makes the search less overwhelming. Think about the property's potential for appreciation, rental income, and overall condition. Your criteria should align with your financial goals and risk tolerance.

Next, outline your financing strategies. This is crucial. You need to know how you're going to fund your investment. Again, to keep things simple, I suggest using a traditional mortgage. Eventually you can consider creative financing options like seller financing or partnerships. Each method has its pros and cons, so weigh them carefully. Make sure you understand the terms and conditions of any loans or financing agreements. This will help you avoid nasty surprises down the road. If you're leveraging existing capital, like using a home equity line of credit (HELOC), ensure you have a clear repayment plan.

Now, establish a timeline for your actions. Setting deadlines for each step keeps you accountable and focused. When do you plan to start your property search? By when do you want to secure financing? Setting these milestones helps break down the process into manageable chunks. This way, you can celebrate small victories along the way, which keeps you motivated. A timeline also creates a sense of urgency, reducing the chances of falling back into analysis paralysis.

Another option is to go with a company that does it all. I use REI Nation and their property management company for the five properties I own that they manage. Keep in mind, YOU still need to keep up with the property managers. Your job is to manage the property managers once you've hired them. There is no "set it and forget it" with ANY investment. However, it's nice to have a good team to help manage all the details, especially if you're buying in cities far from where you live.

REI has everything you need to get started. However, you still have to do your due diligence. You have to decide what areas you'd prefer and do much of the other work listed in this book, but going with a great company like REI Nation is a great way to help cover a lot of the bases.

That said, incorporating risk management strategies into your plan is like having a lifeboat on your ship. You hope you never need it, but it's essential to have it. Diversifying your investments is one way to manage risk. Don't put all your eggs in one basket. Consider investing in different types of properties or even different locations. This way, if one market takes a hit, you're not left high and dry. Employ market analysis techniques to identify emerging trends and potential risks. Regularly review market reports and economic indicators to stay informed.

An example of how I'm managing my risk is the six properties I have are in four locations. Here are the locations: Burbank, CA; Memphis, TN; Fort Worth, TX, and three others near Little Rock, AR. Some areas have been performing better than others, but some also cost significantly less to purchase.

Risk management also involves having contingency plans. What will you do if a property doesn't rent out as quickly as you hoped? How will you handle unexpected repairs? Having answers to these questions can save you a lot of stress and financial strain. Set aside a reserve fund for emergencies. This fund acts as a financial cushion, helping you weather any storms that come your way.

Revisiting and adjusting your plan regularly are two vital components. The real estate market is dynamic, and what worked last year might not work today. Schedule quarterly reviews to assess your progress and make necessary adjustments. Are you on track to meet your goals? Have market conditions changed? Use these reviews to tweak your strategies and stay aligned with your objectives. Flexibility is key. Don't be afraid to pivot if something isn't working. The ability to adapt is a valuable trait in a successful investor.

To help you put all this into action, I recommend using practical tools like investment plan templates and due diligence checklists. Templates provide a structured format for outlining your goals, criteria, and strategies. They ensure you don't miss any critical steps. Due diligence checklists help you thoroughly evaluate properties, ensuring you don't overlook any red flags.

Investment Plan Overview

✓ Define Investment Criteria: Property type, budget, location
✓ Outline Financing Strategies: Traditional mortgage, creative financing, leveraging capital
✓ Establish Timeline: Property search start date, financing secured by purchase date
✓ Risk Management: Diversification plans, market analysis techniques, reserve fund

Creating an actionable investment plan might seem like a lot of work upfront, but trust me, it's worth it. This plan will serve as your roadmap, guiding you through the complexities of real estate investing and helping you stay focused on your goals. And remember, no plan is set in stone. Adjustments are part of the process. The important thing is to start. By laying out a clear plan, you'll find it much easier to take that first step, and each subsequent step will feel less daunting.

So, grab that compass, plot your course, and set sail. The world of real estate investing awaits, and with a solid plan in hand, you're well on your way to success.

2

THE BASICS OF TURNKEY PROPERTIES

Picture this: you've just finished binge-watching a series on Netflix. You know, the one where the protagonist flips houses for a living, turning rundown dumps into sparkling gems. You're pumped, you're inspired, and you think, "I could do that!" But then reality hits. Do you really have the time, energy, or expertise to tackle such a massive project? Probably not, especially if you've got a full-time job, family commitments, or just enjoy your weekends. Enter turnkey properties, the unsung heroes of real estate investing.

WHAT IS A TURNKEY PROPERTY?

A turnkey property is the real estate equivalent of buying a pre-assembled piece of IKEA furniture. It's ready to go, no extra work required. Unlike traditional real estate investments that might need extensive renovations or repairs, turnkey properties are ready-to-rent homes that require minimal to no additional work. Think of it as purchasing a home that's already been spruced up, painted, and polished, just waiting for its new tenant to move in. With turnkey properties, you bypass the stress of dealing with contractors, endless trips to Home Depot, and the uncertainty of renovation timelines.

The process of acquiring a turnkey property is designed to be straightforward, especially when compared to more hands-on investment strategies. First, you need to find a reputable turnkey provider. These companies specialize in sourcing, renovating, and managing properties. They act as one-stop shops, handling everything from the initial purchase to tenant management. As mentioned earlier, my preference is *REI Nation*. They cost the most but do the best with the renovations. Other great choices to consider are *RP Capital, Rent to Retirement*, or you can Google "best turnkey real estate companies" and find what's best for you. However, to keep things as easy and seamless as possible, I suggest starting with *REI Nation* and adjusting accordingly.

Once you've identified a provider, the next step is conducting due diligence. This involves thoroughly researching the company, reviewing their track record, and verifying the condition and value of the property. It's essential to dig deep and ensure you're dealing with a trustworthy provider. After you've done your homework, you move on to finalizing the purchase. This includes negotiating terms, securing financing, and signing the necessary documents. Before you know it, you're the proud owner of a ready-to-rent property.

Turnkey providers play a crucial role in this process. They are the behind-the-scenes magicians who make turnkey investing possible. These companies typically offer a range of services, starting with property sourcing. They search for properties that have the potential to generate steady rental income and appreciate over time. Once they've acquired a property, they handle all necessary renovations and repairs. This might include updating electrical systems, plumbing, painting, and landscaping. The goal is to bring the property up to modern standards and make it attractive to potential tenants.

But the magic doesn't stop there. Turnkey providers often offer property management services as well. This means they handle all of the day-to-day tasks that come with being a landlord. From advertising the property and screening tenants to collecting rent and coordinating maintenance, they've got it covered. This hands-off approach allows you to enjoy the benefits of real estate investing without the headaches of property management.

Let's look at some typical examples of turnkey properties. Imagine a single-family home in a suburban area. It's a charming three-bedroom, two-bathroom house with a fresh coat of paint, new flooring, and updated appliances. The neighborhood is family-friendly, with good schools and parks nearby. This home is ready to welcome its new tenants, and you can start collecting rent almost imme-diately.

To illustrate further, consider the story of Bob, a busy professional with limited time but a keen interest in real estate investing. Bob found a reputable turnkey provider who offered a beautifully renovated single-family home in a growing suburban area. The provider had already vetted tenants, ensuring a steady stream of rental income from day one. Bob's investment required minimal involvement on his part, allowing him to focus on his career while enjoying the benefits of passive income.

Turnkey properties offer an ideal solution for those looking to get started in real estate investing without the hassle of property renovations and management. They provide a ready-to-rent option that minimizes risks and maximizes convenience. So, if you're ready to dip your toes into the real estate market but don't have the time or expertise to manage a fixer-upper, turnkey properties might just be the perfect fit for you.

BENEFITS OF INVESTING IN TURNKEY PROPERTIES

Imagine this: you purchase a property, and almost immediately, you start seeing rental income flow into your bank account. Sounds like a dream, right? That's one of the biggest financial benefits of investing in turnkey properties. These homes are ready to rent out as soon as you close the deal, meaning you can start generating income from day one. It's like getting a new job and receiving your first paycheck the same week. Who wouldn't love that? This immediate rental income helps you quickly recover your initial investment and begin building a steady cash flow, which is a key advantage for anyone looking to dip their toes into real estate investing.

Another financial perk is the potential for appreciation. Turnkey properties are often located in up-and-coming neighborhoods or areas with strong rental demand, which means there's a good chance the property's value will increase over time. This appreciation can significantly boost your overall return on investment. It's like planting a tree today and enjoying its fruit for years to come. While the immediate rental income keeps your cash flow healthy, the appreciation adds long-term value to your investment portfolio. This dual benefit makes turnkey properties an attractive option for both novice and experienced investors.

Let's talk about time-saving aspects. We all know time is money, and in real estate, this couldn't be truer. One of the biggest advantages of turnkey properties is that they save you a ton of time. You don't have to worry about gutting kitchens, replacing roofs, or dealing with pesky contractors. All the hard work has already been done for you. This is a massive relief, especially if you're juggling a full-time job and other commitments. Imagine coming home from work and not having to think about whether the electrician showed up or if the plumber fixed that leak. Instead, you can kick back, relax, and let the property work for you.

Moreover, most turnkey providers offer comprehensive property management services. This means they take care of everything from tenant screening to maintenance and rent collection. It's like having a personal assistant who handles all the tedious tasks, freeing you up to focus on other ventures or simply enjoy your free time. The convenience of having professional management cannot be overstated. It takes a significant load off your shoulders, allowing you to reap the rewards of real estate investing without the usual stress and hassle.

Turnkey properties also come with reduced risk. These properties are thoroughly vetted before they're put on the market. Turnkey providers carefully select properties in stable neighborhoods with high rental demand, minimizing the risk of vacancies and non-payment. Additionally, these providers ensure the properties are renovated to a high standard, reducing the likelihood of unexpected repair costs. It's like buying a certified pre-owned car—you know it's been inspected and is in good condition. This thorough vetting process provides peace of mind and a level of security that's hard to find with other investment methods.

Professional property management further minimizes risk. Experienced managers handle tenant issues, ensuring that your property remains occupied and well-maintained. They also perform regular inspections and address maintenance issues promptly, preventing small problems from turning into costly repairs. This proactive approach helps maintain the property's value and keeps your tenants happy, reducing turnover and ensuring a steady income stream. Knowing that your property is in good hands allows you to focus on growing your investment portfolio or enjoying the fruits of your labor.

Consider the story of Jane, a busy executive who always wanted to invest in real estate but never had the time. She decided to invest in a turnkey property in a growing suburban area. The property was already renovated and had tenants in place. Within months, Jane was receiving steady rental income without lifting a finger. She was so impressed with the ease and profitability of the investment that she went on to purchase two more turnkey properties. Jane's success story is a testament to the benefits of turnkey investing. It shows how these properties can provide immediate returns and long-term growth with minimal effort.

Another investor, Mark, shared his experience with me during an interview. Mark was initially skeptical about turnkey properties, thinking they were too good to be true. However, after doing his research and talking to other investors, he decided to give it a try. Mark invested in a multi-family unit in an urban area. The property was fully renovated and managed by a reputable turnkey provider. Within a year, Mark saw a significant return on his investment and was thrilled with the passive income he was earning. He said, "I never thought real estate investing could be this easy. Turnkey properties have truly changed the game for me."

These testimonials highlight the transformative potential of turnkey properties. They offer a seamless entry into real estate investing, providing financial benefits, saving time, and reducing risks. Whether you're a busy professional, a novice investor, or someone looking to diversify your portfolio, turnkey properties offer a compelling and convenient investment option.

COMMON MISCONCEPTIONS ABOUT TURNKEY INVESTMENTS

Let's bust a myth right off the bat: the idea that turnkey properties are overpriced. Many believe that these properties carry an inflated price tag because they come fully renovated and ready to rent. However, if you dig into the numbers, you'll see a different story unfolding. Imagine taking on a fixer-upper. You'd have to budget for the initial purchase, the cost of renovations, materials, and the labor involved. Not to mention the time and effort it would take to manage the project. Now, compare that to a turnkey property, where all these aspects are taken care of for you. The price you pay includes the convenience and peace of mind that comes with a move-in ready property. When you factor in the hidden costs and potential headaches of DIY renovations, turnkey properties often end up being more cost-effective in the long run.

Another common misconception is that turnkey properties generate lower returns compared to other types of real estate investments. Some investors think that because they're paying for convenience, the returns will be less impressive. But let's look at the facts. Turnkey properties can indeed deliver competitive returns, especially when situated in high-demand rental markets. Take a recent case study, for example. An investor purchased a turnkey single-family home in a growing suburban area. Despite the higher initial purchase price, the property's ready-to-rent condition allowed the investor to start earning rental income immediately. Over a year, the return on investment was comparable to, if not better than, properties that required significant renovations. The key is to focus on the long-term gains, where the combination of rental income and property appreciation can yield substantial returns.

Turnkey investing isn't just for beginners, either. While it's true that turnkey properties offer an accessible entry point for novice investors, seasoned investors can also benefit significantly. Take the testimonial from a seasoned investor named Mike. With years of experience and multiple properties under his belt, Mike turned to turnkey investments to diversify his portfolio. He appreciated the hands-off approach, which allowed him to focus on other ventures while still growing his real estate assets. Mike emphasized that turnkey properties provided him with a steady income stream and reduced the time he had to spend managing his investments. His experience shows that turnkey properties can be a valuable addition to any investor's portfolio, regardless of their level of expertise.

Another myth that needs debunking is that turnkey properties are limited to specific markets. Some folks think that these properties can only be found in certain areas, but that's far from the truth. Turnkey properties are available in diverse markets across the country, from bustling urban centers to quiet suburban neighborhoods. For instance, you can find turnkey properties in cities like Dallas Fort Worth, where the rental market is booming, as well as in smaller towns that offer stable rental demand and lower entry costs. The variety of locations means you can find a turnkey property that fits your investment goals and budget, whether you're looking for high rental yields in a city or long-term appreciation in a suburban area.

Take a look at John, an investor who found a turnkey property in a growing tech hub. The property's prime location attracted young professionals, ensuring a steady stream of tenants and consistent rental income. On the other hand, Sarah invested in a turnkey property in a quaint suburban town known for its excellent schools and family-friendly environment. Both investments were successful, proving that turnkey properties are not confined to a specific type of market but can thrive in various settings.

In summary, turnkey properties offer a range of benefits that debunk several common misconceptions. They can be cost-effective, provide competitive returns, and are suitable for both novice and seasoned investors. Plus, they're available in diverse markets, offering flexibility and opportunities to match your investment goals. Investing in turnkey properties allows you to enjoy the benefits of real estate without the usual hassles, making it a smart choice for anyone looking to build wealth through real estate.

IDENTIFYING THE RIGHT TURNKEY PROPERTY FOR YOU

Choosing the right turnkey provider is crucial to your success. Think of it like choosing a partner for a three-legged race. If they stumble, you both fall. First, look at the provider's track record. How long have they been in business? A provider with a solid history is more likely to be dependable. Check out customer reviews and testimonials. Real feedback from other investors can give you a good sense of what to expect. If previous clients rave about their seamless experience and solid returns, you're probably on the right track. Conversely, if you see a lot of complaints about hidden fees or poor communication, steer clear.

Location, location, location. It's a mantra for a reason. Where your property is located has a huge impact on its profitability. Market demand is a big part of this. You want a property in an area where people want to live. High demand means you'll have an easier time finding and keeping tenants. Look for neighborhoods with good schools, low crime rates, and plenty of amenities like parks, shops, and restaurants. These factors make an area more attractive to potential renters. For instance, a house near a top-rated school will always be in demand among families.

One source I love for selecting a location is BestPlaces.net. It's a one-stop-shop with great data! You'll find important details such as an overview, cost of living, crime rates, people stats, jobs data, education status, economy, etc. All this information is crucial to help make decisions on where to purchase. I'll go into more detail about what I look for to help make decisions on which properties I consider purchasing.

When evaluating a property, once you've decided on a property, there are several key factors to consider. Start with the property condition. Even though turnkey properties are supposed to be ready to rent, it's still important to inspect the house. Check for any signs of wear and tear that might need attention in the near future. Next, consider the rental potential. Is the property in an area with high rental demand? What's the average rent for similar properties in the area? These questions will help you gauge whether the property will provide a good return on your investment. Don't forget to assess the effectiveness of the management team. A good management team will ensure your property stays in top condition and your tenants remain happy. Again, I like *REI Nation/PPMG. PPMG* is the property management company associated with *REI Nation*.

To help you with this evaluation, there are several tools and resources you can use. Real estate investment calculators are incredibly useful. They allow you to input various data points—like purchase price, expected rent, and expenses—and calculate potential returns. Websites like Zillow and Redfin offer these calculators for free. Another valuable resource is online property databases. My favorite website for analyzing properties is *BiggerPockets* (https://www.bigger pockets.com/analysis/rentals/new). These platforms provide a wealth of information about properties, including historical price data, neighborhood statistics, and even estimates for rental income. Websites like Realtor.com and Trulia are great places to start your research.

To make this more tangible, let's walk through an example. Suppose you're considering a turnkey property in a suburban neighborhood known for its excellent schools and low crime rate. The house is in great condition, with new appliances and a recently updated roof. You check the rental potential and find that similar properties in the area rent for around $1,500 a month. Using a real estate investment calculator, you determine that after expenses, you can expect a positive cash flow. The turnkey provider managing the property has stellar reviews, with clients praising their responsive customer service and efficient management.

In sum, choosing the right turnkey property involves a combination of research, intuition, and practical tools. You need to find a reputable provider, ensure the property is in a desirable location, and use all the resources at your disposal to evaluate its potential. With these steps, you'll be well on your way to making a smart investment that provides steady returns and minimal headaches.

The main points of this chapter are that turnkey properties are a fantastic way to get started in real estate investing. They offer immediate rental income, save you time, and reduce risks. By choosing the right provider and property, you set yourself up for success. In the next chapter, we'll dive into financing your first investment, covering everything from traditional mortgages to creative financing options.

3

FINANCING YOUR FIRST INVESTMENT

Picture this: you're standing at the edge of a diving board, staring down at the pool below. You've watched others take the plunge effortlessly, but you're frozen, unsure if you'll sink or swim. Financing your first real estate investment can feel a lot like that. The good news is you don't have to dive in blind. Let's explore the world of traditional mortgages, where we'll find the stability of a lifeguard and the predictability of a well-marked pool lane.

Traditional Mortgages: Pros and Cons

Let's start with the basics. Traditional mortgages are loans provided by banks or mortgage lenders, designed to help you buy a property. These mortgages come in two main flavors: fixed-rate and adjustable-rate. A fixed-rate mortgage offers an interest rate that remains constant throughout the loan term, which typically ranges from 15 to 30 years. This means your monthly payments stay the same, making it easier to budget and plan. On the other hand, an adjustable-rate mortgage (ARM) starts with a lower interest rate for a fixed period (usually 5, 7, or 10 years), after which the rate adjusts annually based on market conditions. ARMs can be attractive initially but come with the risk of rising payments if interest rates increase.

The advantages of traditional mortgages are numerous. First and foremost, they offer predictable monthly payments. With a fixed-rate mortgage, you know exactly what you'll owe each month, which provides peace of mind and financial stability. This predictability is particularly beneficial for long-term planning, helping you avoid the stress of fluctuating payments. Additionally, traditional mortgages often come with lower interest rates compared to other financing options, especially if you have a strong credit score. This can translate into significant savings over the life of the loan. Moreover, traditional mortgages provide a sense of long-term stability, as they are typically structured over 15 to 30 years. This extended period allows you to build equity in your property gradually, contributing to your overall financial growth.

However, traditional mortgages are not without their drawbacks. One of the main challenges is the strict qualification criteria. Lenders scrutinize your credit score, income, and debt-to-income ratio to determine your eligibility. This rigorous process can be daunting, especially for first-time investors who may not have an extensive credit history. Additionally, the lengthy approval process can be frustrating. From submitting your application to closing the deal, the process can take several weeks or even months, requiring patience and persistence. Furthermore, traditional mortgages often require higher upfront costs, including a down payment (typically 20% of the property's purchase price) and closing costs. These expenses can add up quickly, potentially straining your finances before you even get started.

Let's consider some scenarios where traditional mortgages shine. Imagine you're looking to purchase a property in a stable market, like a suburban neighborhood with strong demand for rental homes. In this case, a fixed-rate mortgage offers the predictability and security you need. You'll benefit from stable monthly payments and the peace of mind that comes with long-term financial planning. Alternatively, if you're pursuing a long-term investment strategy, such as holding a property for several decades, a traditional mortgage provides the stability to weather market fluctuations. Over time, you'll build equity in the property, creating a valuable asset that contributes to your overall wealth.

To illustrate, let's look at a specific example. Suppose you're eyeing a charming single-family home in a growing suburb. The property is in excellent condition, with an attractive rental yield. You decide to go with a fixed-rate mortgage, locking in a low interest rate for 30 years. Your monthly payments are predictable, making it easy to manage your budget and plan for future investments. Over the years, the property appreciates in value, and your rental income steadily increases. By the time you've paid off the mortgage, you have a valuable asset that continues to generate passive income.

But what if you're considering an adjustable-rate mortgage? Let's say you find a fantastic deal on a property with a lower initial interest rate through an ARM. For the first five years, your payments are lower, allowing you to allocate more funds towards other investments or improvements to the property. However, you must be prepared for the possibility of rising interest rates after the initial period. If you're confident in your ability to manage potential increases and have a solid exit strategy, an ARM can be a viable option.

In conclusion, traditional mortgages offer a blend of predictability, stability, and potential savings that make them an attractive choice for financing your first real estate investment. By understanding the pros and cons, you can make an informed decision that aligns with your financial goals and risk tolerance. Whether you opt for a fixed-rate mortgage or take a calculated risk with an adjustable-rate mortgage, traditional financing provides a solid foundation for building your real estate portfolio. So, take a deep breath, step off that diving board, and trust that you've got the knowledge and tools to make a splash in the world of real estate investing.

Checklist for Traditional Mortgage Application

- ✓ Credit Score Check: Ensure your credit score is in good shape – 720+ is good. The higher the better.
- ✓ Income Documentation: Gather pay stubs, tax returns, and other income proof.
- ✓ Debt-to-Income Ratio: Calculate your current ratio to ensure it meets lender criteria.

✓ Down Payment: Save at least 20% of the property's purchase price – some deals will require 30% to get a lower interest rate.

✓ Mortgage Pre-Approval: Obtain pre-approval to streamline the buying process.

✓ Property Evaluation: Assess the property's condition and rental potential.

✓ Closing Costs: Budget for additional expenses like appraisal fees, inspections, and title insurance – expect closing costs to be about 3.5-5% of the purchase price, but most get added to the loan.

Creative Financing Options

When you hear the term "creative financing," you might think of some slick, out-of-the-box strategy that only the savvy, seasoned investors use. Well, let's demystify that right now. Creative financing is simply the use of flexible loan structures and alternative funding sources to acquire properties. Unlike traditional financing, which typically involves a conventional mortgage from a bank or lender, creative financing offers more flexibility and can often make deals happen that otherwise wouldn't. It's like opening a toolbox and finding a set of Swiss Army knives instead of just a plain old hammer. These tools allow you to navigate obstacles and seize opportunities that might seem out of reach with conventional methods.

One popular method is seller financing. Here, the seller acts as the lender, allowing you to make payments directly to them instead of going through a bank. This eliminates the need for bank involvement, which can speed up the process and make it easier to close deals, especially for those who might not meet strict bank criteria. However, there's a catch: seller financing often comes with higher interest rates. The seller is taking on more risk, so they'll want to be compensated for it. But if you can negotiate a reasonable rate, this can be a fantastic way to acquire a property without the red tape of traditional loans.

Then there are lease options, which are essentially rent-to-own agreements. You lease the property with the option to buy it at a later date, usually at a pre-agreed price. This method has a low upfront cost, making it accessible if you're short on liquid cash but still want to get into the market. However, lease options can be complex. The agreements need to be carefully crafted to protect both parties, and you'll want to make sure you fully understand the terms before signing anything. Think of it as dating before you marry the property; you get to know it before fully committing.

Partnerships are another powerful creative financing tool. This involves teaming up with another investor or a group to pool resources and share the risks and rewards. Partnerships can be an excellent way to get started if you don't have enough capital on your own. However, remember that partnerships mean shared profits and shared control. You'll need to be comfortable with the idea of working closely with others and making joint decisions. This can be both a pro and a con, depending on your personality and investment style.

Let's look at some real-life examples. Take the case of Tom, who used seller financing to acquire a duplex. Tom had a decent credit score but lacked the hefty down payment required by traditional lenders. The seller, motivated to offload the property quickly, agreed to finance the deal himself. Tom negotiated a fair interest rate and a manageable monthly payment. This arrangement allowed him to get his foot in the door and start generating rental income almost immediately. The higher interest rate was a small price to pay for the opportunity to own the property.

Another example is Jane, who used a lease option to secure a single-family home in an up-and-coming neighborhood. Jane didn't have enough savings for a down payment but saw the potential in the area. She negotiated a lease option with the owner, allowing her to rent the property for two years with the option to buy it at the end of the lease term. During those two years, Jane saved up for the down payment and improved her credit score. By the time the lease ended, she was in a strong position to exercise her option to buy, locking in a favorable purchase price in a now more desirable market.

Lastly, consider Mike and Sarah, who formed a partnership to invest in a multi-family property. Neither had enough capital to go it alone, but together they pooled their resources and split the costs. They also shared the responsibilities of managing the property, leveraging their individual strengths. Mike handled the financials while Sarah took care of tenant relations and maintenance. The partnership allowed them to acquire a larger, more lucrative property than they could have on their own, and they both benefited from the shared income and reduced workload.

Creative financing opens up a world of possibilities, making real estate accessible even when traditional methods seem out of reach. Whether it's seller financing, lease options, or partnerships, these flexible strategies allow you to tailor your approach to fit your unique situation. Each method comes with its own set of pros and cons—but understanding them gives you the tools to make informed decisions and take action. So, don't let conventional barriers hold you back. Embrace creative financing and find the strategy that works best for you.

These alternative ways to finance can work but are also more challenging to pull off. Plus, for most turnkey companies, these alternative ways of financing won't work. With most turnkey deals, you'll need to focus on traditional means and even more specifically, 30-year fixed. Personally, I've only done 30-year fixed term deals since I qualify for them with my partner (my wife).

Leveraging Existing Capital

Leveraging existing capital in real estate investing is like using a trampoline to gain height instead of trying to jump higher on your own. It involves using assets you already own to fund new investments. One common method is using the equity from properties you already own. Suppose you have a home that's appreciated in value; you can tap into that equity to finance the purchase of additional properties. It's akin to turning your home into a financial springboard. Another method is accessing retirement accounts, like a self-directed IRA, to invest in real estate. This way, you're using funds already set aside for the future to grow your wealth even more.

The benefits of leveraging existing capital are significant. For starters, it increases your purchasing power. By using the equity in your current properties or retirement accounts, you can buy more properties than you could with just your savings. This amplification allows you to control a larger portfolio and potentially enjoy higher returns. Imagine having three rental properties instead of just one, each generating income and appreciating in value. That's the power of leverage. Moreover, leveraging allows you to diversify your investments, spreading risk across multiple assets. If one property underperforms, the others can help cushion the blow, providing a more stable financial foundation.

However, leveraging doesn't come without risks. One of the main concerns is the increased debt load. By borrowing against your existing assets, you're taking on additional debt, which means higher monthly payments and more financial obligations. If your properties don't perform as expected, you could find yourself struggling to keep up with these payments. This leads to the risk of over-leverage, where the amount of debt you've taken on exceeds your ability to repay it. Over-leverage can be particularly dangerous during market downturns when property values drop, and rental income might decline. It's like walking a tightrope; a delicate balance is required to avoid falling.

To leverage existing capital safely, consider several strategies. Home equity lines of credit (HELOCs) are a popular option. A HELOC allows you to borrow against the equity in your home, offering a flexible line of credit that you can use for any purpose, including real estate investments. The advantage of a HELOC is that you only pay interest on the amount you draw, giving you control over your borrowing costs. However, it's crucial to have a solid repayment plan in place to avoid accumulating excessive debt.

Another strategy is cash-out refinancing. This involves refinancing your existing mortgage for more than you owe and taking the difference in cash. For example, if your home is worth $300,000 and you owe $150,000 on your mortgage, you could refinance it for $200,000 and receive $50,000 in cash. This cash can then be used to invest in new properties. Cash-out refinancing can provide a substantial amount of capital, but it also increases your mortgage balance and monthly payments. It's essential to ensure that the new investments will generate enough income to cover these additional costs.

Self-directed IRAs are another powerful tool for leveraging existing capital. Unlike traditional IRAs, which limit you to stocks, bonds, and mutual funds, self-directed IRAs allow you to invest in a broader range of assets, including real estate. By using a self-directed IRA, you can tap into your retirement savings to purchase investment properties. The returns on these investments go back into your IRA, growing your retirement nest egg. However, there are strict rules and regulations governing self-directed IRAs, so it's crucial to work with a knowledgeable custodian to ensure compliance and avoid penalties. The custodian I use is Madison Trust, but there are many great self-directed IRA custodians.

To sum up, leveraging existing capital can be a game-changer in real estate investing. This comes with time and works well when adding to your real estate investment portfolio. It boosts your purchasing power, allows for diversification, and can lead to higher returns. But it's not without its risks. Increased debt load and the potential for over-leverage require careful planning and prudent management. By utilizing tools like HELOCs, cash-out refinancing, and self-directed IRAs, you can leverage your existing assets safely and effectively, paving the way for a more robust and profitable investment portfolio.

Securing the Best Interest Rates

When it comes to financing your first real estate investment, securing the best interest rates can feel like striking gold. It's not just about finding a loan; it's about finding the right loan that won't bleed you dry over time. Several factors influence the interest rates you'll be offered, starting with your credit score. Lenders use this three-digit number to gauge your reliability as a borrower. A higher score tells them you're less risky, which could translate into lower rates. Next up is the loan-to-value (LTV) ratio, which compares the loan amount to the property's value. The lower your LTV, the more favorable your interest rate. Finally, economic conditions play a role. Interest rates fluctuate based on the broader economic climate, including inflation rates and the Federal Reserve's monetary policy.

Improving your credit score is like giving yourself a financial makeover. You read about many of these strategies in my book *Simple Investing Plan for a Better Financial Future*. The first 100 requests who provide me a copy of the receipt for this book, I'll send you a free copy of my book *Simple Investing Plan for a Better Future*. Email your receipt and request to Christopher.C4Pub@gmail.com. Also, please include your mailing address, and I'll get you a signed and numbered copy in the mail. Please allow 6-8 weeks for delivery.

Now, back to improving your credit score. Start by paying down your debt. High credit card balances and outstanding loans can drag your score down, so focus on reducing these as much as possible. Correcting errors on your credit report is another crucial step. Mistakes happen, and even a small error can significantly impact your score. Request a copy of your credit report, review it for inaccuracies, and dispute any errors you find. Consistent on-time payments are the bread and butter of a good credit score. Set up automatic payments or reminders to ensure you never miss a due date. Over time, these efforts can raise your score and make you more attractive to lenders.

Shopping around for the best rates isn't just smart; it's necessary. Different lenders offer different rates, and what one lender sees as a risk, another might not. Using mortgage brokers can be incredibly beneficial. These professionals have access to multiple lenders and can help you find the best rates tailored to your financial situation. Online comparison tools are also valuable. Websites like Bankrate and NerdWallet allow you to compare rates from various lenders with just a few clicks. The key is not to settle for the first offer you get. Cast a wide net and see what's out there.

Negotiating lower interest rates might sound intimidating, but it's entirely possible. Start by showing competitive offers. If you've received a lower rate from another lender, use it as leverage. Lenders often match or beat competitors to win your business. Highlighting strong financials is another tactic. If you have a solid credit score, steady income, and low debt-to-income ratio, make sure the lender knows it. These factors can work in your favor during negotiations. Requesting lender incentives is also a good move. Some lenders offer discounts for setting up automatic payments or for being a long-time customer. Don't be afraid to ask about these perks.

Securing the best interest rates is a multifaceted process that requires attention to detail and a bit of legwork. By understanding the factors that influence rates, improving your credit score, shopping around, and negotiating effectively, you can significantly impact your overall financial outcome. Remember, the goal is to minimize your costs and maximize your returns, setting you up for success in your real estate investment endeavors.

In the grand scheme of real estate investing, securing favorable interest rates is one piece of the puzzle. It's a critical step that can save you thousands of dollars over the life of your loan, giving you more capital to invest in future properties. As you move forward, keep these strategies in mind and continue to build on the knowledge you've gained. Next, we'll dive into the nitty-gritty of property selection and evaluation, ensuring you make informed decisions every step of the way.

The easier option: Go with a one-stop-shop at a turnkey company like *REI Nation*. I don't want this to seem like an advertisement for *REI Nation*, because it's NOT. I'm not affiliated with them in any way other than I use them as my turnkey real estate company and for their property management. When I deal with them, they provide the best lenders with the best rates. It's a win-win situation. *REI Nation* also helps to provide a source for homeowners insurance, which is a requirement. I've shopped for better homeowners' insurance, and most others are anywhere between 50-100%+ higher than the option provided by *REI Nation*. This is another reason to go with a quality, top-notch turnkey real estate company, such as *REI Nation*. You still *must* do your research and keep tabs on things but using *REI Nation* helps save me a lot of time and money.

MARKET ANALYSIS TECHNIQUES

Have you ever felt like a detective in an old noir film, piecing together clues to solve a mystery? That's what market analysis in real estate can feel like. Getting the full picture involves a lot of sleuthing, but the reward is well worth it. Understanding market trends is crucial for making informed investment decisions. If you're going to put your hard-earned money into a property, you want to know it's a smart move. Market trends impact property values and influence rental demand, acting as your crystal ball to predict future returns.

Understanding Market Trends

Let's start with why market trends matter. Imagine buying a property without considering the market. You might find yourself stuck with a depreciating asset or a rental property no one wants to live in. Understanding market trends helps you avoid these pitfalls. When you grasp how trends affect property values, you can buy low and sell high, maximizing your profits. It's like having insider knowledge without scandal. Similarly, trends in rental demand tell you where tenants are flocking to, ensuring your property doesn't sit vacant.

Key indicators signal these trends, acting like breadcrumbs leading you to the golden opportunity. Employment rates are a major factor. High employment usually means people have stable incomes and can afford to pay rent. Areas with low unemployment rates often see higher rental demand and property values. Next, consider population growth. When an area's population is increasing, it's a sign that more people need housing, driving up demand for rentals and property prices. Economic development activities also play a role. New businesses, infrastructure projects, and community improvements can turn a sleepy town into a bustling hub, increasing property values and rental demand.

Again, I use BestPlaces.net to find this data. It's also a great one-stop-shop for data. The more you research, the easier it gets to see the best deals, but at some point, you must pull the trigger. Review Appendix 1 below for specific details on what I use to help decide on purchasing a property. Use this as your guide but make it yours. Each investor is different, so you need to decide what's important to you. My focus is on finding low-cost properties in up-and-coming areas that appear to have stability.

Real Life Example: Appendix 1
Step 1 – Research

Analyzing Oak Branch Cir, TN

I searched at https://www.reination.com/property-listings. However, I do look on other turnkey websites, such as Done For You Real Estate and Rent to Retirement, but so far, I've only purchased through REI Nation because they align with my strategy. Recently, I've learned about a turnkey company called *Done for You Real Estate* that I might consider using in the future. Do your research and make your own decision about who you want to use for a turnkey real estate company.

Here's the breakdown of timing from start to finish:

- ✓ When did I start searching for the Oak Branch Cir, TN property? Wednesday, August 14th
- ✓ When did I close on the property? September 13, 2024

Where did I start?

BestPlaces.net – the cost was $89.99 for a year or $9.99 per month. Other websites can be expensive, but I found *BestPlaces.net* to be the best website for the cost.

Here's what I found on the zip code 38135.

Crime: a ranking of 23.8 is good, but these are rare at a low cost. Most of the other properties I purchased through REI Nation are anywhere from 29.8 to 55.3. Do your best to find properties below 50 or if they're above 50, they're trending lower. The property I purchased with a 55.3 crime ranking was trending lower on the crime scale on BestPlaces.net. Plus, I liked other aspects of that property, such as low unemployment, and the area is growing rapidly – the area is Dallas Fort-Worth.

Once I saw that the Crime rate was within my range, I sent an email to my contact at *REI Nation* and asked him to send me the details of the property and all the photos. After seeing the price was within my range and the property looked amazing, I moved on and did more research at BestPlaces.net. Here's what I found.

Job growth: "The job market in 38135 Bartlett, TN is looking promising with an expected growth rate of 20.74%. This is significantly higher than the national average of 30.54%, making it a great location for those seeking employment opportunities. The unemployment rate in 38135 Bartlett, TN is also lower than the national average of 4.1%, at 3.2%. With a growing number of jobs and low unemployment, 38135 Bartlett, TN is an ideal place to find work."

Economic Trends: Unemployment is low, cost of living is low, and the median household income is higher than the national average.

Population Data: Population growth since the year 2000 is moderate, but I like that there the percentage of households that are married is 55.9%. This says this area is stable – I like stability. Most of my other properties have a lower rate than 50%, but the higher the better. Two of the five turnkey properties I purchased have a marriage rate of slightly under 50%. So, don't let a marriage rate below 50% dissuade you.

Other analysis

BiggerPockets (cost: FREE!): I did a full analysis of 3915 Oak Branch Cir West at https://www.biggerpockets.com/analysis/rentals/new. This analysis indicated that the cash flow for the first two years should be about $400/$450 monthly – this does not include property management fees since I'll have $3,000 in concessions. This cash flow is higher than most of my other properties. Other properties earn about $200-$300 monthly cash flow, but that cash flow will increase over time through refinancing and increases in rent.

AreaVibes (cost: FREE!): This offers some good macro data. Understand that no property is "perfect." You have to be willing to be flexible. Through this website, Oak Branch Cir, TN earned a 72/100. I look for anything above 60/100, so 72/100 passed, but I have purchased properties in the 50s if other variables are in alignment with my strategy and research.

Amenities nearby: I search to see if big retailers are nearby, too. Here are the retailers I searched for and their distance to Oak Branch Cir, TN:

- The Home Depot: 7.3 miles
- Walmart: 1.8 miles

- Target: 6.7 miles
- Trader Joes: 15 miles
- Starbucks: 2.6 miles
- Costco/Sams: 7.6 miles

Large retailers spend millions of dollars deciding where to build. This is not a comprehensive list so use these but consider others. All the retailers listed above are within 15 miles of Oak Branch Cir, TN. I'd prefer if the Trader Joes was closer, but all others are within eight miles, so that's a good indication.

Step 2 – Negotiations

How did I negotiate the deal with *REI Nation* and how did I get management fee concessions ($3,000)?

At the time of this purchase, rates were higher than usual compared to 2 years ago. There weren't many buyers at the time due to the high interest rates. This is known as a buyers-market due to the low number of investors purchasing.

When rates are higher, and it's a buyers-market, it's good to ask for concessions – even in a seller-market, it doesn't hurt to ask. The rate was already being brought down two points by the seller to 5.5%, so that wasn't something I could use to negotiate. However, I did ask for $5,000 in management fee concessions. Initially, the seller didn't want to offer any management fee concessions. I countered that I'll move forward with the deal that day if they'll provide $3,000 in concessions. The $3,000 would be enough to cover management fees for about two years. In two years, rents are projected to increase and if rates drop, I can refinance to the lower rate and earn enough to potentially cover the property management fees. They agreed to the offer, and we were off to the races!

Another concession I requested is that since there wasn't a tenant yet, the seller pays the rent until a tenant is in the unit. They agreed to pay the rent until a tenant is paying the rent, so I'll have immediate cash flow that I can put into other investments and build from there.

<u>Step 3 – Take Action</u>

This is the hardest and easiest of all the steps for your first property. Mind you, this was my 5th. Once the research was completed and I was able to get the negotiations to go the way I wanted, there was nothing holding me back. You must be prepared to just say "YES!" when things go your way. Act now and with time, you'll be happy you said yes. The only regret I have about real estate investing (more specifically turnkey real estate investing) is I wish I had started sooner. I wish I could go back in time and tell my younger self to purchase more real estate. Don't be like the younger me and act now! Five years from now, you'll want to send me a thank you note.

<u>Overview:</u>

Oak Branch Cir, TN is my favorite turnkey deal so far, and it's my 5th. I like all my properties, but this one is my best so far. So, keep in mind that your first deal may or may not be your best deal. The more you do, the better you'll get at making these deals. Getting good at anything doesn't happen overnight – your mindset should be all about the long-game. The sooner you pull the trigger the better, so you can learn and grow. You WILL make mistakes, but the more you do, the better you'll get.

The reasons why Oak Branch Cir, TN is my favorite so far is:

- Low crime rate – 23.8 on BestPlaces.net
- High immediate cash flow - $450/mo.
- Low cost for the home, but it did appraise $5,000 less than the offer price – this is the only property I've purchased that appraised lower
- High marriage rate – 55.9%
- Low unemployment rate
- $3,000 in concessions to cover management fees for the first two years
- Immediate rent is paid
- Low interest rate paid down by seller – 5.5%
- Strong job growth
- AreaVibes ranking was 72/100
- Low cost for the property - $190,000

Keep in mind, these deals are rare, so don't expect to get great deals like this all the time. None of my other properties had this many positive aspects to them. However, every other property purchased appraised HIGHER than what I paid. So, I had immediate equity day one.

<u>Final Summary:</u>

Once I found the property, the process started on August 14, 2024 and I closed on September 13, 2024. It took 30 days to complete this wonderful turnkey transaction from start to finish. The best thing about working with *REI Nation* or similar turnkey companies is they take care of everything – not all turnkey companies do this, so be careful if you go with any other company than *REI Nation*. They have great resources for everything from homeowners' insurance to financing options with rates you won't find anywhere else. Not only that, but you'll also have great property management experience with REI/PPMG – they provide a 1-year warranty.

Finally, REI/PPMG has a vested interest in making this a good deal for you. If they don't do well, they don't get paid. **However, you must keep up on things with them**. If something isn't right, tell them. Don't be afraid to let them know if you aren't happy or if something isn't quite right. It's their job to ensure things go smoothly and that you're happy with your new cash-flowing property.

<u>$1,500 REFERRAL PROGRAM</u>

As of this writing, REI Nation offers a referral program. If you decide to move forward with them, visit https://www.reination.com/referearn. However, don't use REI Nation just because of the referral program.

Use the turnkey company that's best aligned with your situation and strategy. $1,500 is not worth it if it's not a fit for what you're trying to accomplish. Plus, they are expensive, but they do a lot. I'd prefer to work with a company that goes above and beyond with the renovations and pay more for better service than pay more in other ways.

Reading market data reports can feel like deciphering an ancient scroll when you first start, but I promise it's worth the effort. Over time, it will get easier and with a lot of practice, the properties you like the most will easily "pop out "and be clear. Housing market reports are a great place to start. These reports provide data on home sales, prices, and inventory levels. Economic forecasts are another valuable resource. They offer predictions about economic conditions that can affect the housing market, such as interest rates and inflation. Real estate market indices compile various data points into a single metric, giving you a snapshot of market health. By combining information from these sources, you can form a comprehensive view of the market.

But how do you interpret all this data? It starts with understanding the basics. When looking at a housing market report, pay attention to trends in home sales and prices. Rising home prices and increasing sales volumes often indicate a strong market. However, if inventory levels are also rising, it could signal that supply is outpacing demand, potentially leading to a slowdown. Economic forecasts help you anticipate changes in the market. For example, if interest rates are expected to rise, it might make borrowing more expensive, cooling down the housing market. Real estate market indices simplify this process by providing a single number that reflects overall market conditions. A rising index suggests a healthy market, while a falling index could indicate trouble.

Staying updated on market trends is like keeping your ear to the ground. Subscribing to real estate newsletters is a great way to get regular updates delivered right to your inbox. These newsletters often include market reports, expert analysis, and investment tips. Following industry blogs and social media accounts keeps you in the loop on the latest developments and opinions. Many real estate professionals share valuable insights and case studies that can help you understand market dynamics. Attending local real estate events is another excellent strategy. These events provide opportunities to network with other investors, learn from experts, and get a feel for the local market.

To make this more actionable, consider creating a simple checklist to stay updated on market trends:

Market Trend Monitoring Checklist

- ✓ Subscribe to Real Estate Newsletters: Sign up for newsletters from reputable sources like BiggerPockets.
- ✓ Follow Industry Blogs and social media: Follow real estate experts and organizations on platforms like LinkedIn and Twitter.
- ✓ Attend Local Real Estate Events: Look for meetups, conferences, and seminars in your area.

- ✓ Regularly Review Housing Market Reports: Set a schedule to review reports from sources like Zillow, Redfin, and the National Association of Realtors.
- ✓ Monitor Economic Forecasts: Keep an eye on forecasts from financial news sites and economic research organizations.
- ✓ Track Real Estate Market Indices: Use tools like the Case-Shiller Home Price Index to monitor market trends.

Understanding and staying updated on market trends is not just a one-time activity but a continuous process. By keeping a finger on the pulse of the market, you can make informed decisions that position you for success. It might seem like a lot of work, but trust me, the payoff is worth it.

Evaluating Location Desirability

When it comes to real estate, location is everything. However, the highest quality locations are usually significantly more expensive, so you must be flexible. It's the secret sauce that can make or break your investment. First, proximity to amenities is a big factor. People love convenience. Properties near grocery stores, parks, restaurants, and entertainment venues are always in demand. These amenities make life easier and more enjoyable, which means tenants are willing to pay a premium for the convenience. See "Appendix 1".

The **quality of local schools** is another crucial element but know that everyone needs a place to live and not all schools can be 9s and 10s. Most of my properties schools are rated at 3-5, but that doesn't make the schools bad. Still, families prioritize good education, so properties in areas with highly-rated schools often see higher demand and better property values. It's like the difference between front-row seats and nosebleed sections at a game, but not everyone can afford front row, so keep that in mind. Safety and crime rates are also pivotal. Nobody wants to live in a neighborhood where they feel unsafe. Lower crime rates (mentioned in Appendix 1) make an area more attractive to potential tenants and buyers, ensuring your property remains desirable. Transportation and infrastructure play a significant role too. Easy access to public transportation, major highways, and airports can make a location more appealing. Good infrastructure means shorter commutes and better connectivity, which can significantly impact rental demand.

Reviewing local crime statistics is another step you can't skip. Websites like *BestPlaces.net, AreaVibes.com, NeighborhoodScout* and local police department websites offer detailed crime data. Look for trends over time to understand whether the area is becoming safer or more problematic. High crime rates can be a red flag, while declining crime rates can indicate a neighborhood on the upswing. Combining these steps gives you a comprehensive view of the neighborhood's desirability.

Emerging markets are like discovering a band before they hit it big. These are areas that show signs of growth and potential but haven't yet reached their peak. Identifying and capitalizing on these markets can lead to significant returns.

Signs of gentrification are one indicator. When you see new cafes, boutiques, and art galleries popping up, it's a sign that the area is attracting more affluent residents. Planned infrastructure projects also signal future growth. If a new subway line or highway expansion is in the works, it can make the area more accessible and desirable.

Increasing property values are another key sign. Look for areas where property prices are steadily climbing. This trend often indicates a growing demand and a promising investment opportunity. Pay attention to local news and government announcements about new developments and community projects. These can provide valuable clues about where the next hot market might be.

Tools for Market Analysis

Imagine you're a treasure hunter, but instead of a map, you have the latest tech gadgets to guide you to the gold. That's what market analysis tools are for real estate investors. They're your high-tech assistants, making the search for the perfect investment a lot less daunting. Let's start with real estate investment software, which is like having a seasoned financial advisor and a savvy market analyst rolled into one. These tools help you analyze potential returns, assess risks, and make data-driven decisions. Popular names like *RealData* and *BestPlaces.net* come to mind. *RealData* offers comprehensive software designed to evaluate properties, forecast cash flows, and determine investment viability. *BestPlaces.net* on the other hand and as mentioned earlier, specializes in providing detailed population growth, crime reporting, and overall analysis on the area, making it easier for you to pick the right property – all for a low cost vs. most real estate analytics tools.

Using real estate investment software might sound intimidating, but it's quite straightforward once you get the hang of it. Let's take *BestPlaces.net* as an example. Once you visit *BestPlaces.net* you can search for data on the property you'd like to consider. Please see Appendix 1 used before to help with deciding to proceed.

Online market analysis platforms are another valuable tool in your arsenal. They offer a user-friendly interface and access to a treasure trove of data. Platforms like *Zillow, Roofstock,* and *Rentometer* provide comprehensive information on property values, rental rates, and market trends. *Zillow's Zestimate* and *Rent Zestimate* tools, for example, use public and user-submitted data to estimate market values and rental prices. This helps you get a ballpark figure of what to expect in terms of income and appreciation. However, with *REI Nation,* they have a boots-on-the-ground team, that will make this easy for you.

In summary, market analysis tools are like having a team of experts working behind the scenes, providing you with the data and insights you need to make informed decisions. Whether you're using real estate investment software like *BestPlaces.net* or online platforms like *Zillow, Redfin, and Rentometer,* these tools simplify the complex process of market analysis. Even if you have a great property management team doing most of the work for you, it's important to still research and know what to expect.

CASE STUDIES IN MARKET ANALYSIS

Let's talk about Joe, an investor who successfully identified a high-growth market. Joe wasn't looking for the glitzy, high-profile cities. Instead, he focused on mid-sized towns with strong job growth and affordable housing. One day, while reading a local business journal, he noticed a tech company planning to open a new office in a small city. Joe dug deeper, analyzing employment rates, population growth, and local amenities. The data pointed to a future boom. He purchased a few single-family homes in the area, which were quickly rented out. Over the next few years, property values soared, and rental demand skyrocketed. Joe's initial homework paid off handsomely.

From Joe's experience, the importance of thorough research becomes evident. He didn't just rely on surface-level information. He examined multiple data sources, talked to local real estate agents, and even visited the city to get a feel for the neighborhood. This kind of in-depth research is invaluable. It's not just about what you read online; it's about combining that information with local insights. Joe's success was a result of meticulous groundwork, proving that knowledge is indeed power in real estate investing.

Then there's Lisa, who debated between urban and suburban investments. Lisa analyzed both markets meticulously. She noticed that while urban properties offered higher appreciation potential, suburban homes provided more consistent rental demand. She chose to diversify, investing in both markets. Her urban properties appreciated rapidly, while her suburban homes generated steady rental income. This strategy of diversification protected her investments from market fluctuations and ensured a balanced portfolio.

From these case studies, one clear lesson emerges: Whether you're focusing on high-growth markets, revitalized urban areas, long-term or short-term rentals, thorough market analysis is your best friend. The common thread among these successful investors is their commitment to deep research and local market knowledge. They didn't just rely on data; they combined it with on-the-ground insights and strategic thinking.

So, what can you take away from these stories? First, always do your homework even though you'll have a great team with your turnkey real estate team. Dive deep into market data, talk to local experts, and visit the areas you're interested in. Second, be adaptable. Markets change, and being able to pivot your strategy can make all the difference. Finally, diversify where possible. Different markets offer different advantages, and spreading your investments can protect you from risks.

By applying the lessons learned from these case studies and information from Appendix 1, you can replicate their success. Start with actionable steps like identifying key indicators, using multiple data sources, and seeking local insights. Adapt these strategies to fit your unique investment goals and market conditions. The goal is to make well-informed decisions that align with your financial objectives and risk tolerance.

PROPERTY SELECTION AND EVALUATION

I magine you're shopping for a used car. You wouldn't just look at the shiny exterior and take the seller's word for it. You'd want to know if it's been in any accidents, if it has a clean title, and whether the engine is in good shape. The same principle applies to selecting a turnkey property. It's not enough to be dazzled by fresh paint and new appliances. You need to dig deeper to ensure you're making a sound investment. Let's explore the red flags that can turn your real estate dream into a nightmare if overlooked.

ESTIMATING PROPERTY VALUE AND POTENTIAL ROI

Estimating property value is like trying to figure out how much a rare baseball card is worth. You have several ways to go about it, and each method gives you a different perspective. Let's start with Comparative Market Analysis (CMA). This approach involves looking at recent sales of similar properties in the same area. Think of it as checking out the going rate for similar items on eBay before you list your own. By comparing properties with similar features, like square footage, age, and condition, you can get a ballpark figure for your property's value. Real estate agents often use CMA to set listing prices, but you can do it too with the right tools.

Another method is the income approach, which is particularly useful for rental properties. This approach calculates the value based on the income the property generates. Imagine you're a landlord, and your property is a mini business. You'll look at the expected rental income, subtract operating expenses, and figure out how much profit you're making. This profit, or Net Operating Income (NOI), is then divided by the capitalization rate (cap rate) to estimate the property's value. The cap rate is essentially the return you expect on your investment. For instance, if the property generates $50,000 in annual NOI and the cap rate is 10%, the property's value would be $500,000.

The cost approach is another way to estimate property value. This method calculates how much it would cost to replace the property if it were destroyed. It's like figuring out the replacement cost for an insurance claim. You start with the cost of building a new, similar property and then subtract any depreciation. This approach is often used for new constructions or unique properties where comparables are hard to find. While it might not be as common for residential investors, it's good to know the basics.

Accurate ROI estimation is crucial for making informed investment decisions. Imagine buying a car without knowing its mileage or fuel efficiency. You'd be flying blind, right? The same goes for real estate. Knowing your potential return on investment helps you decide if a property is worth your time and money. It ensures financial viability and helps you compare different investment opportunities. If you underestimate expenses or overestimate income, you could find yourself in a financial bind. Accurate ROI estimation helps you avoid these pitfalls and make smarter choices.

Calculating ROI involves a few key steps. First, you need to calculate rental income. This is the total income you expect to generate from renting out the property. If you're renting a single-family home for $1,500 a month, your annual rental income would be $18,000. Next, deduct operating expenses. These include property management fees, maintenance costs, insurance, property taxes, and utilities. Suppose your annual operating expenses amount to $5,000. Subtract these from your rental income to get your NOI. In this example, your NOI would be $13,000.

Assessing appreciation potential is the next step. This involves estimating how much the property's value will increase over time. Look at historical data for the area and consider factors like local economic growth, infrastructure development, and neighborhood improvements. Let's say you expect the property's value to appreciate by 3% annually. Combine this with your NOI to get a fuller picture of your ROI. If the property's current value is $200,000, a 3% appreciation would add $6,000 to your annual return, making your total expected return $19,000.

Several tools and resources can help you estimate property value and ROI effectively. Real estate investment calculators are a great starting point. Websites like BiggerPockets and

Zillow offer calculators that let you input various data points to estimate returns. These tools can save you a lot of time and give you a quick snapshot of a property's potential. CMA tools are also invaluable. Platforms like Realtor.com and Redfin provide data on recent sales of comparable properties, helping you perform your own market analysis.

Online property valuation platforms like *Zillow's Zestimate* and *Redfin's Estimate* offer automated valuations based on public data and user inputs. While these estimates aren't always perfect, they provide a useful reference point. For a more detailed analysis, consider using software like *RealData* or *BestPlaces.net*. These platforms offer comprehensive tools for analyzing rental income, operating expenses, and market trends, helping you make well-informed decisions.

By combining these methods and tools, you can accurately estimate property value and potential ROI. This information is crucial for making informed investment decisions and ensuring the financial viability of your real estate ventures.

DUE DILIGENCE CHECKLIST FOR TURNKEY PROPERTIES

Imagine you're about to buy a used car. You wouldn't just kick the tires and call it a day, right? You'd check the mileage, look under the hood, and maybe even bring a mechanic along. The same principle applies to real estate investing. Conducting thorough due diligence is critical for successful investments. Think of it as your safety net, minimizing risks and ensuring you're not walking into a financial trap. Due diligence involves verifying property details, understanding the financials, and making sure everything is above board.

Ignoring this step is like playing Russian roulette with your hard-earned money.

So, what exactly should you be looking at during your due diligence process? First, verify the property title. This is crucial. You need to ensure the seller has clear ownership of the property and that there are no liens or encumbrances. A good turnkey real estate company, such as REI Nation, will do this for you, but you can also purchase title insurance. Some states require title insurance, like the Oak Branch Cir, TN example in Appendix 1.

Inspecting the property's condition is another vital step. Even though turnkey properties are supposed to be ready to go, you should still have an inspection done. This ensures that the renovations were done properly and that there are no hidden issues. An inspector will check everything from the foundation to the roof, giving you a comprehensive overview of the property's condition. **Don't skip this step**; it's your first line of defense against unexpected repair costs.

Let's focus on some key areas that require special attention during due diligence. Property management agreements are crucial. If your turnkey property comes with a property management service, review the agreement carefully. Understand the fees, services provided, and the terms of the contract. You want to ensure that you're getting good value for your money and that the management team is reliable.

Now, let's talk about some real-life examples to illustrate the importance of thorough due diligence. Sarah found a beautiful turnkey property with an attractive price tag. She followed her due diligence checklist, which included a thorough inspection. The inspector discovered that while the property looked great on the surface, it had significant plumbing issues that would have cost a fortune to fix. Armed with this information, Sarah was able to negotiate a lower price, factoring in the repair costs. Her meticulous approach ensured that she didn't overpay and could budget for necessary repairs.

In summary, due diligence is your best friend when it comes to real estate investing. It's a comprehensive process that involves verifying property details, reviewing financial records, and inspecting the property. Pay special attention to property management agreements and compliance with local regulations. By thoroughly vetting a property before you buy, you minimize risks and set yourself up for a successful investment. So, remember to bring your metaphorical mechanic along and check under the hood before making any commitments.

USING PROPERTY INSPECTIONS TO YOUR ADVANTAGE

Imagine you're about to buy a car, but instead of just taking it for a test drive, you bring along a mechanic. That's what a property inspection is like in the real estate world. It's your detailed check-up to ensure everything is in tip-top shape. Property inspections are crucial for making informed investment decisions. They help you identify potential issues and ensure the property's condition matches your expectations. Skipping this step is like driving off the lot without noticing the "Check Engine" light.

The first step in conducting a thorough property inspection is hiring a professional inspector – my team at REI Nation always provides me with a list to help. Look for someone with strong credentials and positive reviews. I visit Yelp.com or do a simple Google search. This isn't the time to skimp; a good inspector can save you a lot of money and headaches down the road.

When reviewing the inspection, focus on key areas like the foundation, roof, and plumbing. The foundation is the backbone of the property. Cracks or shifts can be indicators of major structural issues. The roof is another critical area. Missing shingles or sagging sections can lead to leaks and water damage. Plumbing is equally important. Check for leaks, water pressure, and the condition of pipes. These elements can significantly impact your maintenance costs and the property's overall value.

Common issues found during inspections often include water damage, electrical problems, and pest infestations. Water damage can be a silent killer, leading to mold growth and structural decay. Electrical issues, such as outdated wiring or faulty circuits, can pose safety hazards and complicate financing. Pest infestations, like termites or rodents, can cause extensive damage and be costly to eradicate. Identifying these problems early allows you to address them before they escalate, saving you from unexpected expenses. Most of these issues will be resolved with good turnkey companies, but it's always good to ask questions like "Did your team see any termite damage when renovating?"

Interpreting inspection reports can feel like reading a foreign language, but it's vital for making informed decisions. Start by identifying critical issues. These are problems that need immediate attention and could affect the property's habitability or safety. Next, estimate repair costs. Your inspector might provide rough estimates, but it's wise to get quotes from contractors for accuracy. Finally, use this information to make informed negotiation decisions. If the inspection reveals significant issues, you can negotiate a lower purchase price or request that the seller (aka, the turnkey company) make repairs before closing. *REI Nation* always steps in and fixes any issues right away.

Here's a quick guide to help you stay on track during the inspection process:

Property Inspection Checklist

- ✓ Hire a Professional Inspector: Verify credentials and read reviews.
- ✓ Accompany the Inspector if you have the resources, but I haven't done this due to the credibility and service from REI nation.
- ✓ Key Areas to Inspect: Foundation, roof, plumbing, electrical systems.
- ✓ Common Issues to Watch For: Water damage, electrical problems, pest infestations.
- ✓ Reading the Inspection Report: Identify critical issues, estimate repair costs, make informed negotiation decisions.

Using property inspections to your advantage is all about being proactive and thorough. It's your safety net, ensuring you're fully aware of what you're buying. By identifying potential issues, understanding the property's condition, and interpreting inspection reports effectively, you can make informed investment decisions that set you up for success.

With property selection and evaluation covered, you're now equipped to make smarter, more confident decisions in your real estate investments. Next, we'll delve into the nuts and bolts of managing your turnkey property, ensuring it remains a profitable and hassle-free venture.

HELP OTHERS BUILD WEALTH WITH YOUR REVIEW

YOUR WORDS COULD MAKE A BIG DIFFERENCE

"A small act of kindness can make a world of change."

— UNKNOWN

When we share what we know, we help others grow. If you've enjoyed this journey so far into real estate with me, I'm inviting you to share just a bit of your experience.

Our goal with *Turnkey Real Estate Investing* is simple: to make real estate easy to understand and accessible to everyone who wants to start. But for this book to reach others, it needs more than just a good cover; it needs reviews.

This is where you come in. By leaving a review, you're not only helping others decide to give this book a try, but you're also helping them find a path to financial independence.

Your review, even just a few sentences, could be the encouragement that someone needs to finally act. You could help…

…one more family start building wealth.
…one more person make their first big investment.
…one more future investor learn without costly mistakes.
…one more reader build the life they dream of.

To make a difference, all you need to do is leave a review. It takes less than a minute, but it could help someone make a change that lasts a lifetime.

Click here: https://www.amazon.com/review/review-your-purchases/?asin=B0DMTJF8NF

By taking this step, you're not just a reader; you're a beacon of hope for investors everywhere. Thank you for joining thus far in this journey.

Get ready to dive deeper into strategies, stories, and lessons that will transform your approach to challenges and help you on our path to regular monthly cash flow.

With gratitude,

Christopher A. Stevens

MANAGING YOUR TURNKEY PROPERTY

Imagine you're the captain of a ship, smoothly sailing across calm seas. Everything seems perfect until you realize you've got a stowaway onboard. In the world of real estate investing, that stowaway can be a bad tenant. They might seem fine at first, but soon, they're causing trouble, damaging your property, or skipping rent payments. This is where tenant screening comes into play. It's your first line of defense, ensuring that your investment remains profitable and hassle-free. Keep in mind, most turnkey companies that also offer property management companies take care of the tenant screening – that's why I use REI Nation. It's one less thing to worry about.

Tenant Screening Essentials

First and foremost, let's talk about why tenant screening is so crucial. Think of it as the gatekeeper to your investment. Thorough screening reduces tenant turnover, which means fewer headaches for you. A good tenant will stay longer, saving you the time and expense of finding new tenants every few months. This stability is invaluable, especially when you're trying to maintain consistent cash flow. A bad tenant can be a nightmare, causing property damage that eats into your profits. Proper screening can help you avoid these scenarios by filtering out those who might mistreat your property. Moreover, ensuring timely rent payments is another critical aspect. A reliable tenant pays on time, every time, making your financial planning smoother and less stressful. According to the National Multifamily Housing Council, about nine out of ten tenants pay their rent on time, so thorough screening can help you align with this statistic.

Now, let's dive into the tenant screening process. It all starts with conducting background checks. This step gives you a comprehensive view of a potential tenant's history, including any criminal records. Services like *First Advantage* and *SmartMove* can be invaluable here, providing detailed and up-to-date information. Reviewing credit reports is next on the agenda. A tenant's credit history can tell you a lot about their financial responsibility. Look for red flags like late payments, maxed-out credit cards, or any bankruptcies. Verifying employment and income is also essential. You want to ensure that your tenant has a stable job and sufficient income to cover the rent. Request recent pay stubs or contact their employer directly for confirmation. Finally, don't forget to check their rental history. Speak with previous landlords to get insights into the tenant's behavior and reliability. Were they respectful of the property? Did they pay rent on time? These insights can be invaluable.

Legal considerations in tenant screening are not to be overlooked. Compliance with the Fair Housing Act is paramount. This federal law prohibits discrimination based on race, color, religion, sex, national origin, familial status, or disability. It's essential to treat all applicants equally and base your decisions on objective criteria. Avoiding discrimination goes hand in hand with this. Make sure your screening process is transparent and consistent for every applicant. Properly handling applicants' information is also critical. The Fair Credit Reporting Act governs the use of tenant screening services, ensuring that applicants' information is used fairly and securely. Always inform applicants if you're going to run a background or credit check and get their written consent. Keep their data confidential and secure, and only use it for its intended purpose.

Tenant screening might seem like a lot of work, and it is. As mentioned earlier, you won't need to manage tenant screening if you're using a property management company. However, it's important to understand what's necessary for good tenant screening.

Maintenance and Repairs: What to Expect

Owning a turnkey property means you expect it to be in good shape from the get-go, but that doesn't mean you can sit back and relax completely. There's always some level of upkeep to keep your investment in top condition. Routine maintenance tasks are the bread and butter of property management. Think of landscaping, HVAC servicing, and pest control. These are your regular chores that keep the property looking good and functioning well. Landscaping not only enhances curb appeal but also keeps the property inviting for tenants. Regular HVAC servicing ensures your heating and cooling systems run efficiently, saving you from costly repairs down the line. Then there's pest control. You don't want your tenants sharing their space with unwanted critters.

Emergency repairs are the curveballs that life throws at you. Plumbing leaks, electrical issues, and broken appliances can happen at any time. When a pipe bursts or the electricity goes out, you need to act fast. Having a plan in place for these emergencies can save you a lot of stress and money. All properties purchased through REI Nation are covered with a one-year warranty. After that, it's on you, but PPMG (the property management arm of REI) will take care of any issues. You will have to pay for this, but you won't have to deal with it. Be sure to have an emergency fund available for any issues.

Seasonal maintenance is another important aspect of property management. Each season brings its own set of tasks. In the spring, you might focus on gutter cleaning to prevent water damage. Summer could be the time for inspecting and repairing any roof damage. Fall is perfect for winterizing your property, ensuring pipes are insulated and heating systems are in good shape. Winter might involve checking drafts and ensuring the property stays warm and cozy. By aligning your maintenance tasks with the seasons, you can stay ahead of potential issues and keep your property in excellent condition all year round.

Proactive maintenance is like preventive healthcare for your property. It helps you catch small issues before they become big, expensive problems. Regular inspections and maintenance tasks can identify wear and tear early, allowing you to fix things before they break completely. This proactive approach not only saves you money on costly repairs but also extends the lifespan of property features like roofs, plumbing, and appliances. It's like getting regular check-ups to stay healthy. Plus, keeping your property well-maintained makes your tenants happy. Happy tenants are more likely to stay longer, reducing turnover and ensuring a steady rental income.

Keeping up with all these tasks might seem overwhelming, but a maintenance schedule can help you stay organized. Here's a practical template to get you started:

Maintenance Schedule Template:

- ✓ Monthly Tasks: Check smoke and carbon monoxide detectors, inspect for water leaks, test all appliances, ensure all lights are functioning.
- ✓ Quarterly Inspections: Inspect HVAC filters and replace if needed, check for signs of pest infestation, inspect exterior for any damage.
- ✓ Annual Servicing: Schedule a professional HVAC servicing, clean gutters, inspect and repair the roof, check and refresh caulk and grout in bathrooms.

Again, your property management company will take care of all of these challenges, but you'll need the funds to pay for them.

Budgeting for unexpected repairs is another important aspect of property management. No matter how well you maintain your property, unexpected issues will arise. Set aside a portion of your rental income each month into a reserve fund for these unplanned expenses. This way, you're not caught off guard financially when something needs fixing. Think of it as your property's emergency fund, providing a safety net when things go wrong.

Proactive maintenance and efficient repairs keep your property in top shape, preserve its value, and ensure tenant satisfaction. By staying on top of routine tasks, preparing for emergencies, and budgeting for the unexpected, you can manage your property effectively and enjoy the benefits of a well-maintained investment.

OUTSOURCING PROPERTY MANAGEMENT TASKS

Outsourcing property management can feel like hitting the jackpot in terms of saving time and reducing stress. Let's face it, managing a property isn't always a walk in the park. There are tenant complaints, maintenance issues, and endless paperwork. By hiring a property management company, you can offload these tasks to professionals who know the ropes. This means freer time for you to focus on other things, like finding your next investment or enjoying a round of golf. The stress reduction alone is worth its weight in gold. You no longer must worry about late-night emergency calls or dealing with tenants who refuse to pay rent.

Another major benefit is access to professional expertise. Property managers are seasoned pros who understand the intricacies of rental laws, market trends, and tenant relations. They bring a level of knowledge and experience that can save you from making costly mistakes. For instance, they know how to set the right rental rates through thorough market studies, balancing income and vacancy rates. They also handle the collection and timely deposit of rent payments, ensuring consistent cash flow. With a property manager, you're not just hiring a service; you're gaining a partner who's invested in your property's success. These professionals excel in marketing and advertising properties to reduce vacancy times. They have established vendor relationships, ensuring quality work at competitive prices for maintenance and repairs.

Professional management also enhances tenant relations. A property management company acts as a buffer between you and the tenant, handling all aspects of the tenant-landlord relationship. This includes everything from maintenance requests to conflict resolution. Tenants appreciate having a professional point of contact who can address their needs promptly and efficiently. Happy tenants are more likely to stay longer, reducing turnover and ensuring a steady income stream. Property managers also ensure compliance with local, state, and federal housing regulations, reducing the risk of legal issues. This level of professionalism not only keeps your tenants satisfied but also protects you from potential legal pitfalls.

When selecting a property management company, there are several key criteria to consider. Start by looking at their experience and track record. How long have they been in business? Do they have experience managing properties like yours? A company with a solid history and a portfolio of similar properties is more likely to be dependable. Next, consider their management fees and services offered. While cost is an important factor, it shouldn't be the only consideration. Understand what services are included in their fees. Are there any additional charges for specific tasks? A transparent fee structure is a good sign of a reputable company. Client testimonials and references are invaluable. Reach out to current or past clients to get a sense of their experience. Were they satisfied with the service? Did the property manager effectively handle issues and maintain the property?

Property management services cover a wide range of tasks. Rent collection is one of the primary responsibilities. Property managers ensure that rent is collected on time and deposited into your account. They also handle tenant screening and placement, conducting background checks, verifying employment, and checking rental history to find reliable tenants. Maintenance and repairs coordination is another critical service. Property managers handle all maintenance requests, schedule repairs, and ensure that work is completed promptly and to a high standard. Financial reporting is also part of their job. They provide regular reports detailing income, expenses, and overall financial performance, giving you a clear picture of your property's profitability.

Maintaining a good relationship with your property manager is crucial for a smooth operation. Clear communication of expectations is the foundation. Make sure you're both on the same page regarding responsibilities, processes, and goals. Regular performance reviews are another important practice. Schedule periodic meetings to discuss the property's performance, address any concerns, and make necessary adjustments. Providing timely feedback is essential. If something isn't working, don't wait until it becomes a bigger issue. Address it promptly to maintain a productive relationship. Remember, a property manager is your partner in ensuring the success of your investment. Treat them with respect and openness, and you'll likely see positive results in your property's performance.

Criteria for Selecting a Property Management Company:

- ✓ Experience and Track Record: Look for a company with a solid history and experience managing similar properties.
- ✓ Management Fees and Services Offered: Understand the fee structure and what services are included.
- ✓ Client Testimonials and References: Reach out to current or past clients for their feedback.

By outsourcing property management tunt tasks, you can focus on growing your investment portfolio while leaving the day-to-day operations in capable hands. This partnership can lead to higher profitability and a more enjoyable investment experience.

Building Long-Term Tenant Relationships

You know that feeling when you find a great barber who always gets your haircut just right? You stick with them because they know you, and you trust them. The same principle applies to tenant relationships. Maintaining good relationships with your tenants is crucial for your property's success. First off, reducing turnover rates is a huge benefit. When tenants feel valued and content, they're more likely to stay longer, saving you the hassle and expense of finding new tenants. High turnover can be a major headache, leading to vacant periods that eat into your profits. Good relationships also ensure timely rent payments. If tenants feel respected and appreciated, they're more inclined to pay on time. It's a lot easier to remind someone about a late payment when you've built a rapport with them. Furthermore, happy tenants take better care of the property. They see it as their home, not just a temporary shelter, and are more likely to treat it with respect.

So, how do you foster these positive relationships? Effective communication is key. Regular check-ins and updates can go a long way. A quick email or phone call every few months to ask if everything is okay shows that you care. Addressing concerns promptly is also crucial. If a tenant reports a leaky faucet, don't wait weeks to fix it. Prompt responses build trust and show tenants that their comfort matters to you. Utilizing technology can streamline communication. Tenant portals for maintenance requests, rent payments, and general inquiries make it easier for tenants to reach you and for you to respond. It's like having a digital concierge that keeps everything running smoothly.

Enhancing tenant satisfaction involves more than just fixing things when they break. Offering lease renewal incentives can encourage tenants to stay longer. Consider small perks like a minor rent discount, a gift card, or even a free carpet cleaning service. These gestures show tenants that you value their loyalty. Providing prompt maintenance services is another way to keep tenants happy. Regularly scheduled inspections and maintenance checks prevent issues from escalating and demonstrate your commitment to maintaining a high-quality living environment. Creating a positive living environment also plays a big role. Ensure common areas are clean and well-lit and consider small touches like fresh paint or seasonal decorations. These details can make a big difference in how tenants feel about their home.

Let's look at some real-life examples of successful tenant engagement. Take the case of implementing a tenant feedback system. By regularly soliciting feedback through surveys or suggestion boxes, you can gain valuable insights into what your tenants like and what needs improvement. This not only helps you make better decisions but also shows tenants that their opinions matter. One investor I know started using a simple online survey tool to gather feedback after every maintenance request. The results were eye-opening and led to several small changes that significantly improved tenant satisfaction.

Most good property management companies will do things to ensure tenant satisfaction. However, you can always ask, during the review process, what they do to ensure higher tenant satisfaction.

Building long-term tenant relationships is more than just good business sense; it's about creating a community where people feel valued and respected. By focusing on effective communication, enhancing tenant satisfaction, and fostering a sense of community, you can ensure that your property remains a desirable place to live. This not only benefits your tenants but also contributes to the long-term success and profitability of your investment.

In summary, maintaining positive tenant relationships is key to reducing turnover rates, ensuring timely rent payments, and encouraging property care. By implementing effective communication strategies, offering lease renewal incentives, and creating a positive living environment, you can enhance tenant satisfaction and foster long-term occupancy. Successful tenant engagement, such as feedback systems and community events, further strengthens these relationships, ultimately contributing to your property's success.

Next, we'll explore the financial intricacies of owning a turnkey property, guiding you through budgeting, tax considerations, and maximizing your investment returns.

ETHICAL INVESTING PRACTICES

Imagine you're out for a run in your neighborhood. You wave to your neighbors, admire the well-kept lawns, and feel a sense of pride in your community. Now, picture owning a property that not only adds to this charm but also reflects your values. This is the essence of ethical investing in real estate. It's not just about making a profit; it's about doing so in a way that benefits everyone involved, from tenants to the broader community. Ethical investing means you're not just a landlord; you're a steward of your property and a positive influence in your community.

Principles of Ethical Investing

Ethical investing in real estate is like being the hero in your own story. You're the one making decisions that reflect honesty, transparency, and a commitment to doing the right thing. At its core, ethical investing involves making choices that benefit not just your wallet but also the people and environment around you. It's about being straightforward and fair, ensuring that all your actions reflect integrity.

Honesty and transparency are the bedrock of ethical investing. This means being upfront with tenants about everything from lease terms to rent increases. If you have to raise the rent, communicate why it's necessary and how it will benefit them, perhaps by funding property improvements. Fair treatment of all stakeholders is crucial. Whether it's tenants, contractors, or property managers, everyone deserves to be treated with respect and fairness. This means non-discriminatory tenant selection, ensuring that everyone has an equal opportunity to rent your property regardless of race, gender, or any other characteristic.

Commitment to sustainability is another pillar of ethical investing. This involves making choices that benefit the environment, such as implementing green building practices or using energy-efficient appliances. Not only do these choices help the planet, but they can also reduce utility costs and attract environmentally conscious tenants. For instance, consider the *Community Preservation Corporation (CPC)* in New York, which has financed over 196,000 affordable housing units, significantly reducing homelessness and promoting sustainability.

The are many benefits of adhering to ethical principles in real estate. First, you'll enhance your reputation and build trust within the community. A landlord known for fairness and transparency will attract high-quality tenants who are likely to stay longer and take better care of the property. This leads to increased tenant loyalty, reducing turnover rates and the associated costs of finding new tenants. Long-term financial stability is another significant advantage. Ethical practices can lead to steady rental income and property appreciation over time, as tenants are more likely to renew their leases and the property's value increases due to sustainable improvements.

Let's dig into the key principles that guide ethical real estate investing. Fair pricing practices are essential. This means setting rent at a fair market value, ensuring it's affordable for tenants while still providing a reasonable return on investment. Non-discriminatory tenant selection is also critical. By using consistent criteria for all applicants, you ensure a fair and equitable process. Responsible property management is another cornerstone. This involves maintaining the property to a high standard, addressing maintenance issues promptly, and ensuring a safe and healthy living environment for tenants.

To illustrate, let's look at a real-life scenario. Imagine a landlord who implements green building practices, such as installing solar panels and using energy-efficient appliances. This not only reduces the property's carbon footprint but also lowers utility bills for tenants, making the property more attractive. Or consider a landlord who communicates transparently with tenants about a necessary rent increase. Instead of simply raising the rent, they explain that the additional funds will be used to upgrade the heating system, improving comfort and reducing energy costs. This transparent communication helps tenants understand the reasoning behind the increase and feel more valued.

Case Study: Implementing Green Building Practices

Meet Sarah, a real estate investor who decided to focus on sustainability. She purchased an older property and invested in green upgrades, including solar panels, energy-efficient windows, and a rainwater harvesting system. These improvements not only reduced the property's environmental impact but also lowered operating costs. Sarah marketed the property as an eco-friendly rental, attracting tenants who valued sustainability. The property quickly became a sought-after residence, with high tenant retention and increased rental income.

Ethical investing in real estate is not just a feel-good approach; it's a smart business strategy. By prioritizing honesty, fairness, and sustainability, you build a positive reputation, attract loyal tenants, and achieve long-term financial stability. Whether you're implementing green practices or ensuring transparent communication, ethical principles guide you to make decisions that benefit everyone involved. So, lace up those running shoes, wave to your neighbors, and take pride in being an ethical investor who makes a positive impact.

Building Trust with Tenants and Contractors

Imagine you're hosting a barbecue. You've got your friends, family, and neighbors over. The grill is sizzling, the drinks are flowing, and everyone's having a good time. Now, picture pulling this off if no one trusted you to handle the food, drinks, or even the invite list. It would be a disaster! The same goes for real estate investing. Trust is your secret sauce. Without it, your investment can quickly turn into a messy, stressful ordeal.

Building trust in real estate relationships is crucial for several reasons. For starters, trust leads to fewer disputes. When tenants and contractors trust you, they're more likely to cooperate and less likely to question your decisions. This smooths out many potential conflicts before they even start. Enhanced cooperation from tenants and contractors means things get done more efficiently. If a tenant trusts you, they'll report issues promptly, making it easier for you to address them before they escalate. Contractors who trust you will be more willing to go the extra mile, knowing they'll be treated fairly and paid on time.

Trust is the cornerstone of any successful real estate investment. It reduces disputes, enhances cooperation, and creates a more efficient and enjoyable experience for everyone involved. Whether it's through clear communication with tenants or honoring payment terms with contractors, building and maintaining trust is an ongoing process that pays dividends in the long run. So, fire up that grill, keep the drinks flowing, and make sure everyone at your real estate barbecue feels like they can trust you to deliver.

Long-Term Relationship Building in Real Estate

Think about your oldest friend. The one who's seen you through thick and thin, who you can call at 2 a.m. just to talk. That's the kind of relationship you want to cultivate in real estate. Long-term relationships with tenants, contractors, and property managers are the backbone of a stable and profitable investment. They provide stability and predictability, allowing you to plan your finances without worrying about constant changes. For real estate investors, these long-term ties are like an anchor, keeping you grounded and secure in an ever-changing market.

Maintaining long-term relationships requires effort and commitment. Regular check-ins and updates are a great way to keep the lines of communication open. Whether it's a simple email to your tenants asking how things are going or a quarterly meeting with your property manager to review performance, these touchpoints show that you care and are engaged.

Celebrating milestones and anniversaries is another effective strategy. Remembering a tenant's move-in anniversary with a small gift or card can make a big impact. It shows that you see them as more than just a rent check and appreciate their presence on your property. The same goes for contractors and property managers. Acknowledging the completion of a major project or a year of successful collaboration fosters goodwill and strengthens your professional bond.

Networking plays a crucial role in building and maintaining these relationships. Attending industry events, joining real estate associations, and participating in local meetups are excellent ways to expand your network. These gatherings offer opportunities to meet like-minded individuals, share experiences, and learn from others in the field. Building a strong professional network not only provides support and advice but also opens doors to potential partnerships and investment opportunities. It's like having a safety net of trusted contacts you can rely on when needed.

Let's take a look at some real-life examples to illustrate the power of long-term relationships. Imagine a landlord who has maintained a ten-year relationship with a commercial leaseholder. Over the years, they've built a level of trust and understanding that benefits both parties. The tenant feels secure in their lease, knowing they have a landlord who supports their business. In return, the landlord enjoys a stable, long-term tenant who consistently pays rent and maintains the property. This relationship has saved the landlord time and money by reducing turnover and vacancy rates, all while fostering a positive and supportive environment.

Another example involves a decade-long partnership with a property management company. The investor and the property manager have worked together for years, developing a seamless workflow and mutual trust. The property manager understands the investor's preferences and standards, ensuring that properties are managed efficiently and effectively. This long-term relationship has allowed the investor to focus on expanding their portfolio, confident that their properties are in good hands. The property manager benefits from a steady stream of business and a strong professional relationship, creating a win-win situation for both parties.

The importance of long-term relationships in real estate investing cannot be overstated. They provide stability, predictability, and a sense of community that benefits everyone involved. By maintaining regular check-ins, offering value-added services, celebrating milestones, and actively networking, you can nurture and sustain these relationships for the long haul. Just like your oldest friend, these connections will stand the test of time, contributing to your success as a real estate investor.

Regularly engaging with your tenants and contractors, and acknowledging their contributions, creates a supportive and collaborative environment. This proactive approach helps address issues before they escalate, ensuring a smooth and positive experience for all parties involved.

8

RISK MANAGEMENT STRATEGIES

Imagine you're on a high-wire tightrope, balancing above a bustling city. Below you, life goes on—cars honking, people walking, and somewhere, a dog is barking. Now, there's no safety net, and you're tiptoeing with a mix of excitement and dread. That's what real estate investing can feel like. The stakes are high, and every step matters. But what if I told you that with the right strategies, you could build your own safety net, ensuring that even if you stumble, you won't fall? Welcome to the world of risk management in real estate investing.

Identifying Potential Risks

First, let's talk about the different types of risks you might encounter. Think of these as the various challenges you'll face while walking that tightrope. Market risk is like a sudden gust of wind that can throw you off balance. It encompasses the broader economic cycles that impact property values and rental income. Imagine you've invested in a property during an economic boom, and then a recession hits. Property values could plummet, and rental demand might dry up. This risk is ever-present and can be mitigated by keeping a close eye on economic indicators like job growth, interest rates, and GDP growth.

Then there's property-specific risk, which is like discovering that your tightrope has frayed sections. This includes issues like hidden structural defects or needed renovations that can be costly and time-consuming. Even a turnkey property isn't immune to this risk. Before making a purchase, always hire a professional inspector to uncover any hidden problems. It's better to spend a little upfront than to face massive repair bills down the line.

Tenant risk is another biggie. Imagine a bird landing on your tightrope, causing it to sway. Tenants can be unpredictable—they might miss rent payments, damage the property, or vacate suddenly. Effective tenant screening and strong lease agreements are your best defenses here. A thorough background check can save you from future headaches.

Finally, we have financial risk. This is like realizing halfway across the tightrope that your balance pole is too heavy. Borrowing money to invest can amplify your gains, but it also magnifies your losses if things go south. If your property's income doesn't cover mortgage payments, you could find yourself in a financial bind. Borrow responsibly and always prepare for interest rate changes.

So, how do you systematically identify and evaluate these risks? Enter the SWOT analysis—a simple but powerful tool. SWOT stands for Strengths, Weaknesses, Opportunities, and Threats. Start by listing the strengths of your investment, like its location or quality of tenants. Next, identify weaknesses, such as high maintenance costs or potential legal issues. Opportunities might include market trends favoring rental properties or upcoming infrastructure projects in the area. Finally, assess the threats, such as economic downturns or new regulations that could impact your investment.

Another useful method is creating a risk matrix. Picture a grid where you categorize risks based on their likelihood and impact. For example, a high-likelihood, high-impact risk like a market downturn should be a top priority, while a low-likelihood, low-impact risk like a minor property repair can be lower on the list. This helps you prioritize which risks to address first.

Financial modeling is also crucial. This involves creating detailed financial projections for your investment. By forecasting expenses, rental income, and potential changes in the market, you can better understand how different scenarios will affect your investment. Tools like Excel or specialized real estate software can help you build these models.

Thorough due diligence is the cornerstone of effective risk management. Skipping this step is like walking on a tightrope blindfolded. For example, uncovering hidden structural issues before purchasing a property can save you from massive repair costs. I once knew an investor who bought a seemingly perfect property, only to find out later that the foundation was sinking. The repair costs ate up all his profits and then some. Another case involved zoning compliance issues. A friend of mine bought a property intending to convert it into rental units, only to discover that local zoning laws prohibited such a conversion. These examples highlight the importance of digging deep before making a commitment.

To aid in risk identification and assessment, several tools and resources are available. Risk assessment templates can provide a structured framework for evaluating potential risks. These templates often include sections for identifying risks, assessing their impact, and outlining mitigation strategies. Real estate risk management software can also be invaluable. Programs like *PropertyMetrics* or *RealData* offer comprehensive tools for analyzing risk, forecasting financial performance, and managing your investment portfolio.

Risk Assessment Tools and Resources

- ✓ Risk Assessment Templates: These can help you systematically identify and evaluate risks. Look for templates that include sections for risk identification, impact assessment, and mitigation strategies.
- ✓ Real Estate Risk Management Software: Programs like *PropertyMetrics* and *RealData* offer robust tools for analyzing risk, forecasting financial performance, and managing your investment portfolio. These tools provide detailed insights and help you make informed decisions.

Identifying potential risks is the first step in building your safety net. By understanding and evaluating the various risks associated with real estate investing, you can take proactive measures to protect your investment. Remember, it's not about avoiding risks altogether—it's about managing them effectively so that you can confidently walk that tightrope and reach your financial goals.

DIVERSIFYING YOUR INVESTMENT PORTFOLIO

Imagine you're at a buffet, and instead of heaping your plate with just one dish, you sample a bit of everything. That's the essence of diversification in real estate investing. Diversification means spreading your investments across various assets to minimize risk and enhance stability. By not putting all your eggs in one basket, you create a safety net that can weather market fluctuations. This approach ensures that if one investment underperforms, others can pick up the slack, maximizing your returns and enhancing your overall financial stability.

There are several ways to diversify a real estate portfolio, each with its unique advantages. One effective strategy is to invest in different types of property. For instance, you might own residential properties like single-family homes or apartment buildings, while also dipping your toes into commercial real estate, such as office spaces or retail stores. This mix allows you to benefit from the varying performance cycles of different property types. For example, during an economic downturn, commercial properties might suffer while residential properties remain stable. By holding both, you balance out the risks and rewards.

Geographic diversification is another powerful tool. By spreading your investments across different locations, you protect yourself from regional economic downturns.

Imagine owning properties in both a bustling city and a quiet suburb. If the urban market faces a slump, your suburban properties might still perform well. For example, an investor I know diversified across multiple states, owning properties in Florida, Texas, and Colorado. When Florida faced a hurricane season that impacted rental demand, his properties in Texas and Colorado continued to generate steady income, cushioning the blow.

Diversifying your financing methods can also add another layer of protection. Instead of relying solely on traditional mortgages, consider creative financing options like seller financing, lease options, or partnerships. Each financing method has its pros and cons but using a mix can reduce your exposure to interest rate hikes or changes in lending practices. For example, an investor might use a traditional mortgage for one property, seller financing for another, and partner with other investors for a third. This approach ensures that if one financing method becomes less favorable, the others can help maintain financial stability.

The benefits of a diversified portfolio are numerous. First and foremost, it reduces your exposure to market fluctuations. If one market takes a hit, your investments in other markets can help offset the losses. This balanced approach provides greater financial resilience, allowing you to weather economic storms with less stress. Additionally, diversification creates a more balanced risk and reward scenario. By spreading your investments across different assets, you achieve a smoother, more predictable return on investment. This all comes with time, so don't try to do too much at one time.

Consider the example of an investor who combines residential rentals with commercial properties. By owning both, they benefit from the stability of residential rentals, which tend to have consistent demand, and the potentially higher returns of commercial properties. This blend creates a balanced portfolio that maximizes returns while minimizing risk. Another case study involves geographic diversification across multiple states. An investor with properties in various regions can protect against localized economic downturns, ensuring a steady income stream regardless of regional market conditions.

Picture this: you own a charming duplex in a growing suburban area, a trendy coffee shop in a bustling city, and a small office building in a business district. Each property serves a different purpose, attracts different tenants, and operates in distinct market cycles. When the business district faces a slowdown, your suburban duplex continues to thrive, and the coffee shop caters to loyal customers who never miss their morning brew. This diversified approach ensures that your investments complement each other, creating a robust and resilient portfolio.

The idea of diversification might seem like a lot to juggle, but it's worth the effort. By spreading your investments across different property types, locations, and financing methods, you build a safety net that can withstand market volatility. This approach not only maximizes your returns but also provides peace of mind, knowing that your financial future is secure. So, think of your real estate portfolio like that buffet—sample a bit of everything, and savor the balanced, rewarding experience.

PREPARING FOR MARKET DOWNTURNS

Imagine you're riding a roller coaster. The thrill of the highs is exhilarating, but the sudden drops can be stomach-churning. Market downturns in real estate are much the same. They can hit hard, affecting property values, rental demand, and your overall returns. When the market takes a dive, property values often decrease, making it difficult to sell without incurring a loss. Increased vacancy rates are another common issue. Tenants might lose their jobs or move to more affordable housing, leaving you with empty units and no rental income. Financial strain on cash flow becomes a reality. You still must cover mortgage payments, property taxes, and maintenance costs, but with reduced or no rental income, balancing the books becomes a challenge.

So, how do you prepare for these inevitable downturns? Start by maintaining a cash reserve. Think of it as your financial cushion. Keeping a reserve fund can cover unexpected expenses and tide you over during periods of low rental income. It's like having an emergency fund for your investment property. This reserve should ideally cover three to six months of operating expenses, including mortgage payments, utilities, and maintenance costs. Having this buffer allows you to manage your property without panicking during tough times.

Reducing debt levels is another effective strategy. High debt can be a heavy burden during a downturn. By lowering your debt, you reduce the pressure on your cash flow. Consider refinancing your mortgage to secure a lower interest rate or paying down high-interest loans. This not only improves your financial stability but also provides more flexibility in managing your investment. Securing long-term leases with your tenants can also provide stability. Long-term leases ensure a steady rental income, reducing the risk of vacancies. Offer incentives for tenants to sign longer leases, such as slight rent reductions or property improvements. This creates a win-win situation where tenants feel valued, and you benefit from consistent cash flow.

Diversifying your income streams can further mitigate the impact of market downturns. If you rely solely on rental income from one property, a vacancy or market slump can be devastating. Consider investing in multiple properties or different types of real estate to spread the risk. Additionally, explore other income-generating activities related to your property, such as offering storage space or renting out parking spaces. These additional income streams can help cushion the blow during economic downturns.

Staying informed about market conditions is crucial. Knowledge is power, and being aware of economic indicators and real estate trends can help you anticipate downturns and take proactive measures. Follow economic reports that highlight trends in employment, interest rates, and GDP growth. These indicators provide valuable insights into the overall health of the economy and its potential impact on the real estate market. Attend industry conferences to network with other investors and gain firsthand knowledge from experts. Subscribing to market analysis newsletters keeps you updated on the latest trends and developments. This constant flow of information allows you to make informed decisions and stay ahead of potential downturns.

Consider the case of an investor who successfully navigated a recession. During the 2008 financial crisis, many real estate investors faced significant losses. However, one savvy investor I know maintained profitability by diversifying his portfolio and staying informed. He had properties in both residential and commercial sectors, spread across different states. When the residential market took a hit, his commercial properties continued to generate steady income. Additionally, he had secured long-term leases with his tenants, ensuring a stable rental income despite the economic downturn. His proactive approach allowed him to weather the storm and even acquire new properties at lower prices, positioning himself for future gains.

Another example involves adjusting investment strategies in response to market changes. An investor noticed early signs of an economic slowdown and decided to shift focus from high-end luxury rentals to more affordable housing options. This strategic adjustment attracted a broader tenant base and ensured higher occupancy rates during the downturn. By staying flexible and adapting to changing market conditions, the investor minimized losses and maintained a steady cash flow.

Preparing for market downturns is about building resilience into your investment strategy. By maintaining a cash reserve, reducing debt levels, securing long-term leases, and diversifying income streams, you create a safety net that protects your investment during tough times. Staying informed and adjusting your strategies based on market conditions further enhances your ability to navigate downturns successfully. It's like having a well-designed roller coaster seatbelt—ensuring that even during the steep drops, you remain secure and ready to rise again.

Legal Protections and Insurance

Imagine you're building a castle. It's grand, impressive, and stands tall against the horizon. But what good is a castle without a moat and strong walls to protect it? In real estate investing, legal protections and insurance are your moat and walls. They safeguard your investments, ensuring that unexpected challenges don't bring your financial fortress crashing down.

Legal protections are crucial in real estate investing because they ensure compliance with laws and regulations, protecting you from costly legal disputes. Imagine buying a property and later discovering it violates zoning laws. You'd be stuck in a legal quagmire, facing fines and potentially having to alter or sell the property. Ensuring compliance means doing your homework—checking local zoning laws, understanding tenant rights, and staying updated on any changes in real estate regulations. This diligence helps you avoid legal pitfalls that can drain your resources and peace of mind.

Beyond compliance, legal protections minimize liability. Let's say a tenant slips on an icy walkway in front of your property and decides to sue. Without proper legal safeguards, you could be on the hook for medical bills and damages. Having a solid lease agreement, clear property maintenance protocols, and understanding landlord-tenant laws can protect you against such liabilities. These measures ensure you're not left vulnerable to legal claims that can damage your reputation and finances.

Now, let's talk about insurance. Think of insurance as your financial safety net. It's there to catch you when things go wrong. Property insurance is the most basic form, covering damage to the property itself from events like fire, theft, or natural disasters. Imagine a severe storm damaging the roof of your rental property. Property insurance would cover the repair costs, saving you from a significant financial hit.

Liability insurance is equally important. It protects you against claims if someone is injured on your property. Remember the icy walkway scenario? Liability insurance would cover the tenant's medical bills and legal fees, ensuring you're not out of pocket. This type of insurance provides peace of mind, knowing that you're protected against accidents and injuries that could otherwise lead to financial ruin.

Rent loss insurance is a lesser-known but valuable coverage. It compensates you for lost rental income if your property becomes uninhabitable due to a covered event, like a fire or flood. Imagine a pipe bursts in your property, causing extensive damage that requires months of repairs. Rent loss insurance would cover the lost rental income during this period, helping you maintain cash flow even when the property isn't generating rent.

Umbrella policies offer an additional layer of protection – this is best for newer real estate investors due to the simplicity and low cost. They provide extra liability coverage beyond the limits of your standard policies. Think of it as a backup plan for your backup plan. If a claim exceeds the limits of your liability insurance, the umbrella policy kicks in to cover the excess amount. This coverage is particularly useful for real estate investors with multiple properties, offering broad protection against significant claims.

Having adequate insurance coverage offers several benefits. Financial protection is the most obvious. It ensures that unexpected events don't lead to financial ruin. Whether it's property damage, liability claims, or lost rental income, insurance covers these costs, allowing you to focus on growing your investment portfolio. Insurance also provides peace of mind. Knowing that you're protected against a range of risks reduces stress and allows you to make investment decisions with confidence. Additionally, being properly insured enhances your credibility as an investor. It shows that you're responsible and prepared, which can attract better tenants and more favorable financing terms.

Selecting the right insurance policies requires careful consideration. Start by working with insurance brokers who specialize in real estate. They can help you navigate the complexities of insurance and find policies that suit your specific needs. Be sure to compare policy terms and conditions. Not all insurance policies are created equal, and understanding the fine print is crucial. Look at coverage limits and exclusions to ensure you're adequately protected. For instance, some property insurance policies might exclude certain types of natural disasters, like floods or earthquakes. If your property is in a flood-prone area, you'll need additional flood insurance.

Assessing coverage limits is another important step. Make sure the policy limits are sufficient to cover potential losses. For example, if your property is worth $500,000, ensure your property insurance covers at least that amount. Similarly, check the limits on liability insurance to ensure they're high enough to protect you against significant claims. It's better to have a bit more coverage than you think you need, rather than finding out too late that your policy falls short.

To wrap up, legal protections and insurance are your best defenses in the world of real estate investing. They safeguard your investments, ensuring compliance with laws, protecting against legal disputes, and minimizing liability. Adequate insurance coverage provides financial protection, peace of mind, and enhanced credibility. By working with insurance brokers, comparing policies, and assessing coverage limits, you can ensure that your financial fortress remains strong, no matter what challenges come your way.

9

SUPPLEMENTARY LEARNING AND RESOURCES

Imagine you're sitting in traffic, stuck behind a line of cars that stretches as far as the eye can see. The radio plays the same songs on repeat, and you feel your patience wearing thin. Now, picture this: you pop in your earbuds, hit play on a real estate podcast, and suddenly, your commute transforms into an educational goldmine. You're not just passing time; you're soaking up wisdom from industry experts, gaining insights that could make or break your next investment. Welcome to the world of real estate podcasts—a treasure trove of knowledge that fits in your pocket.

Top Real Estate Podcasts

Podcasts are a fantastic resource for continuous learning and staying updated on market trends. They offer access to expert opinions and advice, all while you go about your daily activities. Whether you're driving, exercising, or cooking dinner, podcasts turn mundane tasks into opportunities for growth. They're like having a mentor on demand, sharing their secrets and strategies whenever you have a moment to listen.

One of the top recommended podcasts is the BiggerPockets Real Estate Podcast. This show is a community-driven power-house, featuring discussions that range from beginner tips to advanced strategies. With hosts who are real estate investors themselves, the podcast dives into practical advice that listeners can apply immediately. Episodes often include interviews with successful investors, providing a blend of inspiration and actionable insights. Imagine listening to a story about someone who started with nothing and built a portfolio of properties—it's both motivating and enlightening.

Next up is The Real Estate Guys Radio Show. These hosts have been around the block, and their experience shines through in every episode. They focus on market analysis and investment strategies, offering deep dives into economic conditions, tax laws, and property management tips. This podcast is perfect for those who want to understand the bigger picture and make informed decisions based on market trends. It's like having a financial advisor and a real estate guru rolled into one, guiding you through the complexities of the market.

For those who crave daily doses of real estate wisdom, there's The Best Ever Real Estate Investing Advice Show. Hosted by Joe Fairless, this podcast features daily episodes with industry experts who share their best advice. The format is fast-paced and packed with value, making it ideal for busy individuals who want to learn something new each day. You'll hear from a diverse range of professionals, from flippers and wholesalers to landlords and developers. It's a smorgasbord of expertise that keeps you coming back for more.

Another gem is the Real Wealth Show, hosted by Kathy Fettke. This podcast focuses on building wealth through real estate, with a strong emphasis on creating passive income streams. Kathy's approachable style and genuine passion for helping others make this show both informative and enjoyable. Topics range from market updates and investment strategies to personal finance tips and success stories. It's like having a friendly chat with a knowledgeable friend who wants to see you succeed.

To get you started, here are some specific episodes that are particularly insightful for beginners. On the BiggerPockets Real Estate Podcast, check out the episode titled "How to Get Started in Real Estate Investing." This episode breaks down the basics in a way that's easy to understand, offering practical steps to take your first plunge. For those interested in market dynamics, The Real Estate Guys Radio Show has an episode called "Understanding Market Cycles." This deep dive into how market cycles work will help you time your investments more effectively.

If creative financing intrigues you, don't miss the episode "Creative Financing Techniques" on The Best Ever Real Estate Investing Advice Show. It's a treasure trove of alternative funding strategies that can open up new possibilities for your investments. Each episode is like a masterclass, offering nuggets of wisdom that can significantly impact your real estate journey.

So, whether you're stuck in traffic, hitting the treadmill, or simply relaxing at home, tune into these podcasts. They're a gateway to expert advice, real-world success stories, and practical tips that can help you overcome analysis paralysis and make informed decisions in your real estate ventures.

Other podcasts that will help with real estate and diversification of your portfolio are Money Ripples by Chris Miles and Done for You Real Estate by Kevin and Steve. Money Ripples is my "go to" podcast to learn. I never miss an episode and often times I'll listen to the same one multiple times.

Online Communities for Real Estate Investors

Imagine you're at a bustling marketplace. Every stall has something unique to offer, and the more you explore, the more treasures you uncover. That's what online communities for real estate investors are like. They're vibrant spaces filled with people eager to share their knowledge, experiences, and secrets to success. Joining these communities can provide immense support, networking opportunities, and valuable insights that can propel your real estate investing journey.

One of the biggest benefits of these communities is peer support and encouragement. When you're feeling stuck or overwhelmed, a quick scroll through a forum can reveal others who have faced similar challenges and overcome them. You'll find encouragement from seasoned investors who've been in your shoes and come out the other side. This camaraderie can be a powerful motivator, helping you push through doubts and keep moving forward.

Access to a wealth of shared knowledge and experiences is another significant advantage. Online communities are like a living library of real estate wisdom. Members share their success stories, mistakes, and lessons learned along the way. You can find detailed case studies, property analysis, and even step-by-step guides on various investing strategies. This collective knowledge can save you from costly mistakes and accelerate your learning curve.

These communities also offer opportunities for collaboration and partnerships. You might find someone looking to co-invest in a property, or perhaps a mentor willing to guide you through your first deal. Collaborations can provide you with the resources, capital, and expertise you might lack on your own. It's like assembling a superhero team, each member bringing their unique strengths to achieve a common goal.

Now, let's talk about some of the top online communities for real estate investors. The BiggerPockets Community is a heavyweight in this space – look me up and follow me and I'll follow you back. It boasts extensive resources and active discussions on virtually every real estate topic. From forums and blogs to podcasts and webinars, BiggerPockets offers a treasure trove of information. The community is incredibly active, with members eager to answer questions, provide feedback, and share their experiences. It's like having a 24/7 support group that's always ready to help.

The Reddit Real Estate Investing Forum is another valuable resource. Reddit's diverse range of topics and user experiences makes it a unique platform. You'll find threads on everything from beginner questions to advanced strategies.

The community is known for its candid and often humorous discussions, making it a fun and engaging place to learn. Real estate memes, anyone?

Real Estate Investment Groups on Facebook offer real-time interactions and local meetups. These groups are often more localized, allowing you to connect with investors in your area. This local focus can provide insights into specific markets, trends, and opportunities that broader communities might overlook. Plus, the real-time nature of Facebook allows for quick responses and dynamic discussions.

LinkedIn Real Estate Networking Groups cater to professional networking and industry insights. These groups are more formal and business-oriented, providing opportunities to connect with industry leaders, potential partners, and mentors. Discussions often revolve around market analysis, investment strategies, and professional development. It's an excellent platform for building a robust professional network and staying updated on industry trends.

To get the most out of participating in these online communities, consider a few tips. Start by asking questions and seeking advice. Don't be afraid to post your queries, no matter how basic they might seem. The community members are there to help, and you'll often find that others have the same questions. Sharing personal experiences and insights is equally important. Your unique journey and lessons learned can provide valuable perspectives for others. Plus, sharing your successes and challenges can foster deeper connections and build your reputation within the community.

Building connections and networking with other members is crucial. Engage in discussions, comment on posts, and reach out to individuals who share your interests or goals. Networking isn't just about what you can gain; it's also about what you can offer. Be generous with your knowledge and support, and you'll find that others are more willing to reciprocate. Plus, the more you share, the more you'll learn.

Online communities are a treasure trove of support, knowledge, and opportunities. Dive in, explore, and connect. The insights and connections you gain can be the difference between feeling stuck and moving forward with confidence.

Further Reading and Educational Resources

Imagine you're at a bookstore, surrounded by shelves filled with titles promising to unlock the secrets of real estate success. You pull out a book, flip through the pages, and feel a surge of excitement at the knowledge within your grasp. Continued reading is crucial in this ever-evolving industry. Staying updated on industry trends, learning from experts, and enhancing your knowledge and skills can set you apart from the competition. It's like having a secret weapon in your back pocket, ready to deploy whenever needed.

One must-read book is "Rich Dad Poor Dad" by Robert Kiyosaki. This classic isn't just about real estate; it's about a shift in mindset. Kiyosaki contrasts the financial philosophies of his two "dads"—one rich, one poor. The rich dad emphasizes the importance of investing and building passive income streams. This book will change how you think about money and investing, encouraging you to see opportunities where others see obstacles. It's a foundational read that prepares you mentally for the challenges and rewards of real estate investing.

Next on the list is *The Millionaire Real Estate Investor* by Gary Keller. This book is a treasure trove of strategies for building wealth through real estate. Keller breaks down the process into three parts: Think a Million, Buy a Million, Own a Million. Each section is packed with actionable advice, from setting goals and evaluating properties to structuring deals and managing a portfolio. This book is like having a mentor guide you through every step, ensuring you build a solid foundation for your investments.

The Book on Rental Property Investing by Brandon Turner is another essential read. Turner, a co-host of the BiggerPockets podcast, delves into the nitty-gritty of managing rental properties. He covers everything from finding the right property and screening tenants to handling maintenance and maximizing rental income. Turner's practical tips and real-world examples make complex concepts accessible, helping you navigate the challenges of being a landlord with confidence.

Along with the book you're currently reading, *Micro Wins to Millions – The Moneyball Real Estate System* by Kevin Clayson and Steve Carl is a great read. It will help you with groundbreaking, simple ways to build success, not just in real estate, but in life and money, too. Their stories, lessons, and messages in the book are inspiring.

Beyond books, online courses offer valuable insights and learning opportunities. Platforms like Udemy and Coursera provide courses on various aspects of real estate investing, from finance and property management to market analysis and legal considerations. These courses allow you to learn at your own pace, fitting education into your busy schedule. Real estate investment blogs, like the BiggerPockets Blog, offer a wealth of articles, tips, and case studies from experienced investors. These blogs keep you updated on the latest trends and strategies, providing a steady stream of inspiration and knowledge.

Industry publications, such as *REALTOR* Magazine, offer in-depth articles on market trends, legal issues, and investment strategies. Subscribing to these publications ensures you stay informed about the latest developments in the industry, helping you make well-informed decisions. They are like having a constant pulse on the real estate market, guiding your investment choices with current information.

Let's highlight some key takeaways from these recommended readings. *Rich Dad Poor Dad* teaches the importance of financial literacy and investing, encouraging a shift from earning to building wealth. *The Millionaire Real Estate Investor* provides strategies for building a robust real estate portfolio, emphasizing goal setting, property evaluation, and deal structuring. "The Book on Rental Property Investing" offers practical tips for managing rental properties, ensuring you maintain profitability and minimize hassles. *Micro Wins to Millions – The Moneyball Real Estate System* explores techniques for successful turnkey real estate investing and provides valuable life lessons.

Imagine diving into these resources, soaking up the wisdom of experts, and applying their strategies to your investments. Each book, course, and article add another layer of knowledge, equipping you with the tools to navigate the complex world of real estate. Whether you're a novice investor or looking to expand your portfolio, continued reading and education are your keys to success.

Networking Opportunities in Real Estate

Imagine walking into a room buzzing with conversation, where every handshake could lead to your next big investment. That's the power of networking in real estate investing. Building a strong network is vital for success because it opens doors to new opportunities and deals that you might never find on your own. Networking lets you tap into the collective wisdom of experienced investors who've been through the trenches and come out the other side. You learn from their mistakes, gain insights into their strategies, and even find potential partners for future collaborations. It's like having a cheat code for your investment game.

Real estate investment clubs are a fantastic starting point for building your network. These clubs bring together like-minded individuals who share a passion for real estate investing. They often host regular meetings, workshops, and guest speakers, providing a platform to exchange ideas and learn from others. It's a great way to meet investors at all stages of their journey, from newbies to seasoned pros. Industry conferences and expos are another goldmine for networking. Events like the ICC Summit or NAR NXT, The Realtor Experience, attract top producers, coaches, and industry leaders. These gatherings are packed with interactive sessions, keynote speeches, and opportunities to mingle with experts. Local meetups and workshops offer a more intimate setting to connect with investors in your area.

These events often focus on specific topics, allowing you to dive deep into areas of interest and build relationships with local professionals. Online networking platforms like LinkedIn are also invaluable. They provide a virtual space to connect with industry leaders, join relevant groups, and participate in discussions. It's like having a global networking event at your fingertips, available anytime.

Attending networking events comes with a plethora of benefits. For starters, you gain insider knowledge that's not readily available through books or online resources. Experienced investors often share tips and tricks they've learned over the years, giving you a competitive edge. These events also help you find potential mentors and partners. A seasoned investor might take you under their wing, offering guidance and support as you navigate your first investments. Partnerships can also emerge from these connections, allowing you to pool resources and expertise for larger deals. Perhaps most importantly, networking events can lead to discovering investment opportunities you wouldn't have found otherwise. Someone might mention an off-market property, or you might hear about a promising new development. These nuggets of information can turn into lucrative deals, making your attendance well worth the effort.

To network effectively, preparation is key. Start by crafting a compelling elevator pitch. This is a brief, engaging summary of who you are, what you do, and what you're looking for. Keep it concise but impactful, so you can quickly capture the interest of potential contacts. When engaging in conversations, ask insightful questions. Show genuine interest in the other person's experiences and insights. Questions like, "What's the best investment you've made?" or "What's a lesson you've learned the hard way?" can open up rich discussions and help you learn from their journeys. Following up with new contacts is crucial. After an event, send a quick email or LinkedIn message thanking them for their time and reiterating your interest in staying connected. This simple gesture can solidify the connection and keep the lines of communication open. Leveraging social media for networking is also a smart move. Share valuable content, engage with posts, and join relevant groups to expand your reach and build your online presence.

Networking isn't just about collecting business cards or LinkedIn connections. It's about building meaningful relationships that can support and propel your real estate investing endeavors. Each conversation, handshake, and follow-up email are steps toward creating a robust network that can provide guidance, opportunities, and partnerships. So, whether you're attending a local meetup, joining an investment club, or participating in an industry conference, approach each interaction with curiosity and openness. The connections you make today could be the catalysts for your success tomorrow.

EXIT STRATEGIES

Imagine you're at a massive buffet (yes, we're back at the buffet), and you've been piling your plate with all your favorite dishes. You're about to dig in when you realize—maybe, just maybe—you've bitten off more than you can chew. Finding an exit strategy in real estate is a bit like knowing when to leave the buffet line. You've enjoyed the ride, but now it's time to cash in your chips and walk away with a smile. Selling your investment property can be a strategic move, whether you're looking to capitalize on gains, free up capital, or simply avoid future market downturns. Let's break down the process.

Selling Your Investment Property

First things first—you need to prepare the property for sale. Think of it like staging a house for a glamorous open house. You'll want to make sure everything is in tip-top shape. Start by decluttering and cleaning the property. A sparkling clean home creates a great first impression. Address any minor repairs that might put off potential buyers—leaky faucets, chipped paint, or squeaky doors.

Your property management company can help with getting your property ready for sale and they'll offer suggestions for an agent. Do your research, but most good property management companies will have your back and take care of a lot of the heavy lifting.

Once you've selected an agent, it's time to list the property. This involves more than just snapping a few photos and throwing them online. High-quality photos are a must—consider hiring a professional photographer. A well-written listing description that highlights the property's best features can also make a big difference. If you really want to stand out, consider creating a virtual tour. In today's digital age, many buyers start their search online, so making a strong first impression is crucial.

Now comes the fun part—negotiating with buyers. Be prepared for offers to come in below your asking price; it's all part of the game. Your agent will help you navigate the negotiations, ensuring you get the best possible deal. Remember, it's not just about the price. Consider other factors like the buyer's financing, contingencies, and closing timeline. Sometimes, a slightly lower offer with fewer contingencies can be more attractive than a higher offer with lots of strings attached.

You might wonder why selling could be the best exit strategy. For starters, selling allows you to realize capital gains. If your property has appreciated significantly since you bought it, you can cash in on that increased value. This influx of capital can be used for new investments, paying off debts, or even a well-deserved vacation. Selling can also free up capital for new investments. Maybe you've got your eye on a new opportunity that promises even better returns. By selling your current property, you'll have the funds to seize that next big deal. Moreover, selling can also help you avoid potential market downturns. If you sense that the market is cooling off, selling now can help you lock in your gains before prices start to drop.

Of course, selling isn't without its costs. Real estate agent commissions are typically the biggest expense, usually around 5-6% of the sale price. Closing costs can also add up, covering things like title insurance, escrow fees, and transfer taxes. Don't forget about capital gains taxes. If you've owned the property for more than a year, you'll pay long-term capital gains tax, which is generally lower than short-term rates. Lastly, any repairs and staging costs will come out of your pocket. However, these expenses can often be recouped through a higher sale price.

Selling your investment property can be a strategic and profitable move. By preparing the property, hiring a skilled real estate agent, listing it effectively, and negotiating wisely, you can ensure a smooth and successful sale. Remember the benefits of realizing capital gains, freeing up capital for new investments, and avoiding potential market downturns. Be aware of the associated costs and take steps to maximize your sale price. Now, let's get that property sold and move on to your next great investment adventure!

Refinancing for Better Terms

Refinancing might sound like a fancy financial maneuver, but at its core, it's pretty straightforward. Refinancing means replacing your existing mortgage with a new one, ideally with better terms. Think of it as trading in your old clunker for a shiny new car with better gas mileage. The main goal is to secure a lower interest rate, which can save you a bundle over the life of the loan. It's all about tailoring the mortgage to better suit your current financial situation.

The benefits of refinancing can be significant. One of the most appealing advantages is reducing your monthly payments. Lowering the interest rate on your loan means you'll pay less interest each month, freeing up more cash for other expenses or investments. Another perk is accessing the equity you've built up in your property. This can be a great way to get funds for new investments or home improvements. Improved cash flow is another big plus. With lower monthly payments, you'll have more disposable income, which can be used to pay down other debts or reinvest in your property.

So, how do you go about refinancing? The process starts with evaluating your current loan terms. Take a close look at your interest rate, loan balance, and remaining term. Compare these with current market rates to see if refinancing makes sense. Next, shop around for the best refinance rates. Don't just settle for the first offer you get; compare multiple lenders to find the best deal. Once you've found a lender with favorable terms, you'll need to submit a refinance application. This involves providing documentation like pay stubs, tax returns, and information about your property. After your application is approved, you'll move on to closing the new loan. This step involves signing the final paperwork and paying any closing costs associated with the refinance.

To make the refinancing process smoother, there are a few tips you should keep in mind. First, improving your credit score before applying can help you secure better rates. Pay down existing debt, correct any errors on your credit report, and make sure all your bills are paid on time. Next, compare multiple lenders. Different lenders offer different rates and terms, so shopping around can save you a lot of money. Also, be aware of the costs and fees associated with refinancing. Closing costs can add up, so make sure you understand all the fees involved and factor them into your decision. Finally, timing the refinance is crucial. Market conditions can impact interest rates, so keep an eye on trends and try to refinance when rates are low.

Refinancing can be a powerful tool for real estate investors. By securing better terms on your mortgage, you can reduce your monthly payments, access equity, improve cash flow, and lock in stable interest rates. The process involves evaluating your current loan, shopping for the best rates, submitting an application, and closing the new loan. With careful planning and attention to detail, you can navigate the refinancing process effectively and come out ahead.

Holding Properties for Long-Term Gains

Holding onto an investment property long-term can be like nurturing a fine wine—it gets better with age. The benefits of this strategy are numerous and can significantly outweigh the challenges. One of the most compelling advantages is appreciation potential. Over time, properties in desirable locations tend to increase in value. This appreciation can lead to substantial profits when you eventually decide to sell. Imagine buying a property for $200,000 and seeing its value rise to $400,000 over a couple of decades. That's a cool $200,000 in your pocket without lifting a finger.

Consistent rental income is another major perk. Holding a property long-term allows you to benefit from steady rental payments, providing a reliable stream of income. This can be especially valuable during retirement when you're looking for passive income. Additionally, rental income can help cover mortgage payments, property taxes, and maintenance costs, making the investment self-sustaining. The longer you hold the property, the more likely it is that rental rates will increase, further boosting your income.

Tax benefits also make long-term holding attractive. As a property owner, you can deduct expenses such as mortgage interest, property taxes, and repairs from your taxable income. Depreciation is another significant tax benefit. Even though your property may be appreciating in value, the IRS allows you to depreciate the property over time, reducing your taxable income. When the time comes to sell, you can benefit from lower long-term capital gains tax rates. Moreover, if you decide to reinvest the proceeds into another property, a 1031 exchange can help you defer capital gains taxes.

Equity buildup is yet another advantage. As you pay down your mortgage, you build equity in the property. This equity can be tapped into for future investments or used as collateral for loans. Over time, the combination of mortgage paydown and property appreciation can lead to significant equity, enhancing your overall net worth. Think of it as a forced savings plan where your tenants are helping you build wealth.

However, holding properties long-term isn't without its challenges. Market volatility is a significant concern. Economic downturns can lead to declining property values and rental rates. While real estate generally appreciates over the long term, short-term fluctuations can be nerve-wracking. Property management responsibilities can also be demanding. Dealing with tenant issues, maintenance requests, and repairs can be time-consuming and stressful, especially if you own multiple properties.

Maintenance and repair costs are another downside. Over time, properties require upkeep, and these costs can add up. From replacing roofs to fixing plumbing issues, ongoing maintenance is necessary to keep the property in good condition. Tenant turnover is yet another challenge. Finding and retaining good tenants can be difficult. High turnover rates can lead to vacancy periods, lost rental income, and additional costs for cleaning and repairs between tenants.

Despite these challenges, many investors have successfully navigated the long-term holding strategy. Take, for instance, a case study of a property purchased in a growing suburb 20 years ago. Initially bought for $150,000, the property's value steadily increased due to the area's development and rising demand. Today, it's worth $500,000. Throughout the years, consistent rental income covered the mortgage and maintenance costs, while strategic upgrades like energy-efficient windows and a modernized kitchen attracted high-quality tenants. The owner now enjoys substantial equity and a significant increase in net worth.

Another example is an investor who focused on generating steady cash flow through long-term rentals. By carefully selecting properties in stable neighborhoods with high rental demand, they ensured a reliable income stream. Regular maintenance and proactive property management kept tenants happy, resulting in low turnover rates. Over time, rental rates increased, further boosting cash flow. This consistent income allowed the investor to reinvest in additional properties, gradually building a diversified portfolio.

Holding properties for the long term can be highly profitable. With the potential for appreciation, consistent rental income, tax benefits, and equity buildup, it offers numerous advantages. Strategies like regular maintenance, strategic improvements, effective property management, and reinvesting rental income can enhance long-term gains. While challenges like market volatility, management responsibilities, maintenance costs, and tenant turnover exist, successful examples demonstrate the significant rewards of this strategy.

Planning Your Exit Strategy

Ever watched a magician pull off a flawless disappearing act? One moment, something's there, and poof—it's gone. That's the kind of finesse you want in your exit strategy for real estate investing. Having an exit strategy isn't just smart; it's crucial. Think about it. You wouldn't jump out of a plane without a parachute, right? Planning your exit ensures you meet your financial goals, minimize risks, and adapt to changing market conditions.

Setting clear financial objectives is your starting point. Know what you want to achieve. Are you looking to maximize profits, free up capital, or diversify your portfolio? Your goals will shape your exit strategy. For example, if your aim is to maximize profits, you might decide to sell when the market is high. If freeing up capital is your priority, refinancing could be your go-to move. Your objectives act as your compass, guiding every decision you make.

Considering tax implications is also essential. Capital gains taxes, depreciation recapture, and other tax considerations can affect your net returns. Consulting with a tax advisor can help you navigate these complexities. For instance, a 1031 exchange allows you to defer capital gains taxes by reinvesting the proceeds into another property. Understanding these tax implications helps you make informed decisions and maximize your after-tax returns.

Tax Hive is a great source for helping with bookkeeping, tax strategy, tax filing, and much more. Without this kind of assistance, running your business will be stressful and difficult. So, if you don't have a good source for keeping your books and taxes organized, set up a meeting with a Tax Hive representative to see if their services are a good fit for you.

Transitioning smoothly from planning your exit strategy, the next chapter will delve into real-life success stories and case studies. These examples will provide valuable insights and inspiration, highlighting how strategic planning and execution can lead to remarkable outcomes in real estate investing. So, gear up for some real-world wisdom that will further empower you on your investment journey.

REAL-LIFE SUCCESS STORIES AND CASE STUDIES

Imagine standing at the edge of a cliff, peering down at the churning waters below. Your heart is pounding, your palms are sweaty, and every logical part of your brain is screaming to step back. But then, you see someone take a leap, splashing safely in the water. As they reach the surface, you can see them grinning ear to ear. That's what real estate investing can feel like for first-timers—terrifying yet exhilarating. Let's dive into some real-life stories to show you that taking that leap is not only possible but can also be incredibly rewarding.

Success Stories from First-Time Investors

Take Sarah, for instance. She was a Senior Product Designer from the bustling San Francisco Bay Area, where real estate prices often feel like a cruel joke. Determined to invest, Sarah turned her gaze to Memphis, where the numbers made more sense. She invested in a single-family rental property, leveraging turnkey services to manage the renovations and tenant placements. Her first year brought a net cash flow of almost $3,000, with a cap rate of 8.4% and a gross yield nearing 14%. It wasn't all smooth sailing—she faced the fear of market downturns and the challenges of managing her property remotely. But by relying on a solid property management team and staying informed about market trends, she turned her initial investment into a steady source of passive income.

Then there's David, who wrestled with analysis paralysis for months. He had the capital but was paralyzed by the fear of making a mistake. David's breakthrough came when he attended a local real estate meetup, where he connected with a mentor who had been in the game for decades. This mentor introduced him to the concept of creative financing, specifically seller financing, which allowed David to purchase his first property without the daunting upfront costs. David's journey was filled with challenges, from tenant issues to unexpected maintenance costs. However, he tackled these hurdles head-on by maintaining open communication with tenants and building a network of reliable contractors. His first property not only became profitable but also gave him the confidence to invest in more.

These stories highlight the importance of leveraging turnkey properties and creative financing to get started. Both Sarah and David faced significant challenges—Sarah with the fear of market downturns and David with tenant issues. They overcame these obstacles through thorough due diligence and effective management strategies. Sarah made sure to vet her property management team thoroughly, while David built a robust network of contractors and mentors.

For you, the actionable takeaways are clear. Thorough due diligence is non-negotiable; it's your first line of defense against potential pitfalls. Networking and mentorship are invaluable—having someone who's been through the trenches can provide insights that no book or online course can. Finally, don't let the fear of the unknown hold you back. Every successful investor started where you are now, and the only way to move forward is to take that leap.

Overcoming Challenges: Real Investors' Journeys

Maria's story is a stark reminder that real estate isn't always smooth sailing. She bought a promising turnkey property, thinking it would be a hassle-free investment. But soon after, she encountered the tenant from hell. This tenant not only missed multiple rent payments but also caused significant damage to the property. Maria found herself entangled in a legal battle over eviction. It was a stressful period, but she had a great property management company to help. They had everything she needed to hire an attorney to get the tenant removed promptly despite attempts at helping the tenant.

A month later, after the tenant was removed the property management company assessed the damage, cleaned up the property and got it ready to rent. The following month, she had a new tenant who paid on time and got her back on track to regular cash flow.

For you, the lessons are clear. Always have a contingency plan. Unexpected issues will arise and having a backup strategy can save you from financial ruin. Build a reliable support network, whether it's a great property management company, a trusted contractor, or a seasoned mentor. These connections can provide guidance and assistance when you need it most. Finally, maintain a positive mindset and stay adaptable. Real estate investing is a marathon, not a sprint. Challenges will come, but with the right strategies and support, you can overcome them and achieve your investment goals.

A Real-Life Challenge with My First Property Through REI Nation

Like Maria's story and other real estate investors, I faced challenges with a tenant shortly after purchasing my first property through REI Nation. After receiving four months of rent payments, the tenant began to struggle and couldn't pay rent on time. Both PPMG, my property management company, and I made every effort to work with the tenant, as eviction was the last thing I wanted. The tenant remained in communication and made partial payments, but gradually fell further behind. After three months of attempting to catch up, the tenant eventually stopped answering calls from PPMG and refused to make any more payments.

With mortgage payments still due every month and no rental income, I was losing thousands of dollars. Despite my reluctance, we had to initiate the eviction process. Thankfully, PPMG stepped in and managed everything. They promptly started the legal process and hired an attorney for a minimal cost to handle the paperwork.

Due to a court backlog, the eviction in Arkansas took about eight weeks (normally, it takes half that time). Once PPMG confirmed the tenant had vacated, they quickly addressed all necessary repairs and cleaning to prepare the property for the market. In less than six weeks, the property was listed and rented to a new tenant.

While the ordeal cost about $12,000 in lost rent and repairs, the property is now occupied by a reliable tenant, and I'm optimistic about things moving forward. This was my first —and hopefully last—eviction.

Key Takeaways from My Experience

- *Be prepared: This experience taught me the importance of having reserves. Unexpected situations happen, and financial preparedness is key.*
- *Stay positive: Even in challenging circumstances, maintaining a positive mindset helps navigate tough decisions.*
- *Long-term perspective: Despite the setbacks, I believe this property will prove to be a valuable investment over time.*
- *Trust your team: PPMG was a game-changer—they handled every aspect of this stressful process, allowing me to focus on the bigger picture.*

Ultimately, what could have been an overwhelming situation was made manageable thanks to PPMG's support.

Lessons Learned from Experienced Investors

Let's talk about Susan, a veteran real estate investor with 30 years of experience. She's seen markets rise and fall, yet she's managed to navigate these waters with remarkable success. Susan started her career in real estate almost by accident. She bought her first property, a fixer-upper, with the intent of flipping it. However, she quickly realized the value of holding onto properties for long-term gains. Over the years, Susan has built a diverse portfolio that includes single-family homes, multi-family units, and even some commercial properties. Her journey offers invaluable insights for anyone looking to make real estate a serious part of their financial strategy.

One of the most critical lessons Susan has learned is the importance of market analysis and due diligence. Before she makes any investment, she dives deep into market trends, property values, and neighborhood dynamics. She once spent six months studying a particular market before deciding to invest. This rigorous approach has saved her from making costly mistakes and has allowed her to capitalize on opportunities that others might have overlooked. Susan also emphasizes the importance of effective property management. She believes that a well-managed property not only retains its value but also attracts high-quality tenants. Susan has developed a system for regular maintenance checks and tenant screenings, ensuring that her properties remain in top condition and her tenants are happy.

For newcomers, Susan's advice is straightforward: start small and scale gradually. She recommends beginning with a single-family home or a small multi-family unit to get a feel for the demands and rewards of property management. Leveraging professional networks and resources is another piece of her advice. Susan's network of real estate agents, contractors, and fellow investors has been instrumental in her success. She suggests joining local real estate investment groups and attending industry conferences to build a robust support system. And if you don't have time for all that, to get started faster, consider a good turnkey and property management company like REI Nation/PPMG. Susan's approach to diversifying her portfolio is another key take-away. She doesn't put all her eggs in one basket; instead, she spreads her investments across various property types and geographic locations. This strategy has provided her with a stable income stream and reduced her exposure to market volatility.

Navigating multiple market cycles has taught Susan the value of patience and timing. During the 2008 financial crisis, she held onto her properties, confident that the market would eventually rebound. Her patience paid off, as her properties appreciated significantly in the following years. Susan's experience underscores the importance of staying informed and adaptable. Markets change, and successful investors must be willing to adjust their strategies accordingly. Her story is a testament to the power of knowledge, resilience, and strategic planning in real estate investing.

Scaling Up: From One Property to Multiple Investments

Imagine Mike, a young professional who dipped his toes into real estate by purchasing a modest single-family rental property from REI Nation. Initially, he was thrilled just to see a steady stream of rental income. But soon, he caught the bug. One property turned into two, and before he knew it, Mike was managing a portfolio of ten rental properties. His journey from a single property to a diversified portfolio didn't happen overnight. It required strategic planning, reinvesting rental income, and leveraging partnerships.

Mike's first step was to reinvest his rental income into new properties. Rather than splurging on luxuries, he focused on growing his portfolio. Each month's rental income that came from PPMG (Premier Property Management Group) was meticulously saved and pooled to fund his next investment. This disciplined approach allowed him to purchase additional properties without relying excessively on external financing. As his portfolio grew, he also began leveraging partnerships and joint ventures. By teaming up with like-minded investors, Mike was able to spread risks and pool resources, making it easier to acquire larger and more lucrative properties. These partnerships not only provided financial benefits but also brought diverse expertise to the table, enhancing the overall management and growth of his investments.

Scaling up, however, came with its own set of challenges. Managing multiple properties isn't a walk in the park. Mike had to balance property management responsibilities, ensuring that each property was well-maintained, and tenants were satisfied. This is where professional property management services from PPMG became invaluable. By outsourcing day-to-day management tasks, Mike was able to focus on strategic growth rather than being bogged down by maintenance calls and tenant issues. Ensuring consistent cash flow across his investments was another hurdle.

Diversifying property types and locations helped mitigate risks and stabilize income.

For those looking to scale their real estate portfolios, strategic planning and goal setting are paramount. Clearly define your investment goals and develop a roadmap to achieve them. Utilize professional property management services to maintain the quality of your investments and ensure tenant satisfaction. Reinvest your rental income wisely and consider forming partnerships to expand your financial resources and expertise. Scaling up is not just about acquiring more properties; it's about growing sustainably and strategically. By following these practical steps, you can turn a single investment into a thriving portfolio, just like Mike did.

Ethical Success Stories in Real Estate

Let's talk about Emily, a real estate investor who decided to take the path less traveled—ethical investing. Emily wasn't just in it for the money; she wanted her investments to make a positive impact. She focused on sustainable property development. One of her projects was a dilapidated building in a quiet neighborhood. Instead of opting for the cheapest renovations, she chose to implement green building techniques. Solar panels, energy-efficient windows, and a rainwater harvesting system were just a few of the features she added. Emily's commitment to sustainability didn't go unnoticed. Her properties became highly sought after, attracting tenants who valued eco-friendly living, resulting in higher rental rates and lower vacancies.

Emily didn't stop at green building techniques. She also prioritized fair and transparent tenant relations. She communicated openly about rent increases, explaining how the extra funds would go towards building improvements that would benefit everyone. She set up a tenant advisory council to gather feedback and address concerns. This approach fostered a sense of community and trust, which isn't just good karma—it's good business. Tenants who feel valued are more likely to stay long-term, reducing turnover and ensuring a stable income stream. Emily's properties often had waiting lists, a testament to her ethical approach.

The positive impacts of Emily's ethical investing extended beyond her properties. The local community benefited from her sustainable practices and tenant engagement. Her projects led to enhanced community well-being, making the neighborhood more attractive and vibrant. The long-term tenant loyalty she built meant fewer vacancies and higher retention rates, which translated to consistent cash flow. This stability allowed her to focus on expanding her portfolio while maintaining her ethical principles. Emily's success story shows that doing good and doing well aren't mutually exclusive. By prioritizing sustainability and fair practices, she not only achieved financial success but also made a meaningful impact on her community.

If you're considering incorporating ethical principles into your real estate investments, start by prioritizing sustainability and environmental responsibility. Implement green building practices where possible and opt for energy-efficient appliances and materials. Engage in fair and honest business practices by being transparent with your tenants and involving them in decision-making processes. Not only does this build trust, but it also fosters a sense of community and belonging. Ethical investing might require a bit more effort upfront, but the long-term benefits—both financial and societal—are well worth it.

Final Motivational Thoughts and Next Steps

As we wrap up this chapter, let's reflect on the invaluable lessons these stories have offered. The first takeaway is the importance of perseverance and adaptability. Every investor we've discussed faced challenges that could have easily derailed their progress. Yet, they adapted, stayed the course, and turned obstacles into opportunities. Whether it was overcoming tenant issues or navigating high-cost markets, their resilience paid off. Another key lesson is the value of ethical and community-focused investing. These investors didn't just focus on profits; they aimed to make a positive impact. This approach not only enriched their communities but also built long-term trust and loyalty, which is priceless in the world of real estate.

Now, it's your turn. The most crucial step you can take is to set clear and actionable goals. Know what you want to achieve, whether it's securing your first property, increasing your cash flow, or making a community impact. Continuously seek education and improvement. The real estate market is ever-changing, and staying updated will give you a competitive edge. Engage with professional networks and resources. Surround yourself with like-minded individuals who can offer guidance, support, and opportunities. Your network is your net worth; never underestimate the power of connections.

Creating an actionable investment plan is your roadmap to success. Outline your financial goals, identify target properties, and set timelines. Break down each step into manageable tasks. This not only makes the process less daunting but also keeps you on track. Engage with professional networks —join real estate investment groups, attend seminars, and seek mentorship. These connections will provide both knowledge and moral support, helping you navigate the complexities of real estate investing.

Challenges are inevitable, but they are also opportunities for growth. Embrace them with a positive mindset. Remember, every successful investor started where you are now. Believe in your potential for success. The stories we've shared are not just tales of triumph; they are roadmaps showing you that success is achievable, even if the path is filled with hurdles. Every challenge you face is a step towards becoming a seasoned investor.

So, take that leap. Set your goals, create your plan, and start your investment journey with confidence. The next chapter will guide you through advanced strategies to ensure you're not just surviving but thriving in the real estate market.

CONCLUSION

Alright, folks, we've journeyed together through the rollercoaster that is real estate investing. From the first tentative steps of overcoming analysis paralysis to the final leap of creating a solid exit strategy, you've armed yourself with the knowledge to take on the world of turnkey properties. So, let's quickly recap the main points of your new real estate playbook.

✓ We began with Chapter 1, where we tackled the dreaded analysis paralysis. Think of it as staring at a menu with too many options, and instead of drooling over the possibilities, you freeze. We discussed setting clear investment goals using the SMART framework, and how continuous learning can build your confidence. You're not alone in this; even seasoned investors like me once faced the same overwhelming data dumps.

✓ Chapter 2 introduced you to the concept of turnkey properties. Like a pre-assembled IKEA couch, turnkey properties are ready to go, saving you from the headaches of renovations. We covered how to find reputable turnkey providers and the benefits of immediate rental income, minimal involvement, and reduced risk. You met Bob, who turned his busy professional life into a stream of passive income with his first turnkey property.

✓ In Chapter 3, we dove into financing your first investment. We explored traditional mortgages and creative financing options like seller financing and lease options. You learned about leveraging existing capital through methods like HELOCs and cash-out refinancing. The focus was on navigating the sometimes-choppy waters of financing with confidence.

✓ Chapter 4 turned you into a market detective, teaching you how to analyze real estate trends and evaluate location desirability. You discovered tools like real estate investment software and online market analysis platforms. We shared case studies like Joe's high-growth market identification, highlighting the importance of thorough research and adaptability.

✓ Chapter 5 was all about property selection and evaluation. Think of it as shopping for a used car—you wouldn't just kick the tires.

We identified red flags, explained how to estimate property value and potential ROI, and provided a due diligence checklist. Property inspections became your best friend in ensuring you're not buying a lemon.

✓ In Chapter 6, we navigated property management. From tenant screening essentials to handling maintenance and repairs, and outsourcing property management tasks, you learned how to keep your ship sailing smoothly. Building long-term tenant relationships and maintaining open communication were key takeaways.

✓ Chapter 7 emphasized ethical investing practices. We discussed how honesty, transparency, and sustainability can boost your reputation and tenant loyalty. Real-life examples, like Emily's green building practices, showed the long-term benefits of ethical investments.

✓ Chapter 8 was about risk management strategies. We identified potential risks and discussed the importance of diversification and preparing for market downturns. Legal protection and insurance were highlighted as your safety nets. Real-life examples illustrated how to navigate these challenges effectively.

✓ In Chapter 9, we explored supplementary learning and resources. From top real estate podcasts to online communities and essential reading, you now have a treasure trove of knowledge at your fingertips. Networking opportunities were emphasized as crucial for learning and growth.

✓ Chapter 10 focused on exit strategies. Whether you're selling your investment property, refinancing for better terms, or holding properties for long-term gains, having a well-thought-out exit plan is essential. Real-life examples showed how strategic exits can maximize your returns.

✓ Finally, Chapter 11 brought real-life success stories and case studies, showing you that taking the leap into real estate investing is not only possible but can be incredibly rewarding. Sarah, David, and others shared their journeys, highlighting the importance of perseverance, adaptability, and the power of networking.

KEY TAKEAWAYS

1. Overcoming Analysis Paralysis: Set clear goals and continuously educate yourself to build confidence.
2. Turnkey Properties: These are ready-to-rent gems that save you time and reduce risks.
3. Financing: Understand your options, from traditional mortgages to creative financing.

4. Market Analysis: Be a detective; know the trends and the desirability of locations.
5. Property Evaluation: Do your due diligence and rely on property inspections.
6. Property Management: Effective tenant screening and maintenance are key to smooth sailing.
7. Ethical Investing: Honesty, transparency, and sustainability pay off in the long run.
8. Risk Management: Diversify and prepare for downturns with legal protections and insurance.
9. Continuous Learning: Leverage podcasts, books, and online communities for ongoing education.
10. Exit Strategies: Plan your exit to maximize returns and minimize risks.

CALL-TO-ACTION

So, what's next? It's time to take action. Flush that analysis paralysis down the toilet and start setting those investment goals. Dive into the world of turnkey properties and explore financing options that work for you. Keep your detective hat on for market analysis and always do your due diligence when evaluating properties. Build solid relationships with other real estate professional and property managers, and never forget the importance of ethical investing.

FINAL INSPIRATIONAL THOUGHTS

Remember, every successful investor started where you are now—on the edge, peering down at the unknown. But here's the thing: the leap is worth it. The challenges you face will only make you stronger, and the rewards will be sweeter than you ever imagined. Believe in yourself, trust the process, and take that first step. You've got this!

With the tools and knowledge you've gained from this book, you're not just another investor. You're a confident, informed, and ethical real estate investor ready to make a difference. So go ahead, take the plunge, and let your real estate journey begin. Happy investing!

Finally, reach out to me at Christopher.C4Pub@gmail.com if you have any questions or need help, please contact me. My goal is to serve and help people, so please don't hesitate to reach out. Together, we can do BIG THINGS!!!

ACTION ITEM LIST – USING REI NATION

Listed below are all the steps, but if you're going through REI Nation, you can **sidestep** (see highlighted areas) MANY of these items in the process, saving you a lot of time and money. Here's your guide:

<u>1. Educate Yourself</u>

- Research the Basics: Understand the fundamentals of turnkey properties, such as what they are, the benefits, and the potential risks. Now that you've finished this book, you have a good understanding of this.
- ~~Understand Local Real Estate Laws: Familiarize yourself with the real estate market in your target area, including taxes, landlord-tenant laws, and property regulations.~~

REI Nation has a law team that will help. It will still cost money, but they have the resources and experience to help you with this. Based on my experience with evictions and other legal challenges, REI Nation has your back.

<u>2. Set Financial Goals</u>

- Determine Your Budget: Calculate how much you can afford to invest, considering the cost of the property. ~~down payment, closing costs, and potential maintenance expenses.~~
- ~~Assess Financing Options: Explore various financing options, such as traditional mortgages, home equity loans, or private funding. Pre-qualify for a mortgage to know your purchasing power.~~

When you make an offer on a property through REI Nation, they have negotiated contracts with lenders who specialize in turnkey real estate investors. I haven't found better rates or fees from other lenders, so I don't waste my time searching.

Regarding maintenance expenses, REI Nation has a one-year warranty with the buyer when you purchase property from them. You'll have to investigate the details of the warranty, but anything that has gone wrong with a property (which isn't much or often) they've fixed it at no cost.

- Calculate Cash Flow and ROI: Estimate the monthly cash flow by factoring in rental income, mortgage payments, insurance, property management fees, and maintenance. Aim for positive cash flow and an acceptable return on investment (ROI). What's an acceptable ROI? My properties earn from 9%-14% annual ROI over five years. Use this tool to help: https://www.biggerpockets.com/analysis/rentals/new

3. Choose a Location

- Research Real Estate Markets: Look for markets with strong rental demand, affordable property prices, and economic growth. Consider factors like job opportunities, population growth, and crime rates.
- Pick a Stable Neighborhood: Prioritize neighborhoods with good school districts, amenities, and low vacancy rates.

This is limited to the properties available at REI Nation. They have properties in areas where I like to purchase and have done extensive research on where to purchase. If you're interested in a property at REI Nation, ask them: Why did the REI Nation team select this area and property? They'll tell you why and you can decide if it's a good fit for you. I like to purchase in southern states where the cold climate isn't quite as severe.

4. Find a Reputable Turnkey Provider

- Do Thorough Background Checks: Research turnkey providers that have a good track record and positive reviews from other investors. Request references from past clients.

- Inspect Properties and Review Portfolios: Ensure the provider has a history of delivering high-quality, ready-to-rent properties in good condition. Verify that properties meet safety and legal standards.

This is a must. Do your own research and decide what's best for you. While I'm a fan of REI Nation, my next purchase might be with Done for You Real Estate. They align with my strategy as well and they might be a good option for my next purchase.

5. Conduct Due Diligence on the Property

- Order a Home Inspection: Have a professional inspect the property to ensure it's in good condition and there are no hidden repair issues.
- Verify Tenant Information: If the property is already rented, review the lease agreements, tenant history, and rent payments to ensure steady cash flow.
- Review Financials: Get detailed information on the property's income, expenses, and net operating income (NOI).

6. Hire a Property Management Company

- Research Property Managers: A good property manager can handle tenant relations, repairs, and rent collection. Choose a company with local expertise and a solid reputation.
- Agree on Fees and Services: Discuss the management fees, which typically range from 8-12% of monthly rent, and ensure the contract covers all necessary

~~services like tenant screening, maintenance, and reporting.~~

REI Nation's property management company is PPMG – the property management company. The key to managing property management is you MUST check things regularly. When you start, create a checklist of things you have concerns about. First check weekly. Once things get on track, you'll only need to check monthly. Send a note of any concerns or questions to your representative and they'll get back to you. They will inadvertently charge you for things they shouldn't and it's your job to say something.

7. Secure Financing **(see details about financing under Financial Goals above)**

- Finalize Mortgage Details: If you're financing the property, complete your loan application and finalize the terms with your lender. ~~Make sure to lock in your interest rate.~~
- Review Loan Documents: Carefully read through the loan documents before closing, ensuring you understand the terms and conditions.

8. Close on the Property

- Sign the Purchase Agreement: Review the terms of the purchase agreement, including the price, closing date, and contingencies.
- Complete the Closing Process: ~~Work with a title company or attorney~~ **(REI Nation will select a title**

company). Finalize the transaction, pay the necessary closing costs, and transfer ownership.

9. Manage the Investment

- Monitor Performance: Regularly review the financial performance of your investment, including cash flow, expenses, and overall return.
- Maintain Communication with Property Manager: Keep an open line of communication with your property manager to ensure the property is well-maintained and tenants are satisfied.

This is a must, as highlighted under 6. Hire a Property Management Company. Especially when you first get started, keep on top of things daily, if necessary. Yes, it will take some time to get things settled, but once you get things on track, you won't spend much time at all managing the property managers. Two of the five properties I own through REI take me less than an hour a month. Once the other three are on track, I'll spend about one hour a week on all five properties.

10. Plan for Future Investments

- Reinvest Profits: Use the cash flow or appreciation from your first property to invest in additional turnkey properties.
- Expand Your Portfolio: Diversify by acquiring more properties in different locations or types (e.g., single-family homes, multifamily units) to spread risk and increase returns.

By following these steps, you can make a smart, well-informed turnkey real estate investment and start generating passive income. Look for future books from me as I learn more, read them and apply them. This will help save you hours of time and a lot of money.

Now, LET'S GO!

REFERENCES

How to Overcome Real Estate Analysis Paralysis https://www.mashvisor.com/blog/real-estate-analysis-paralysis/

How to Overcome Your Fear of Investing https://www.youtube.com/watch?v=RbAdbSrrdgE

8 Psychological Traps Investors Should Avoid https://www.investopedia.com/articles/investing/060513/avoid-these-common-investing-psychology-traps.asp

Set real estate goals you can crush — here's how https://www.followupboss.com/blog/real-estate-goals

BiggerPockets Review: 7 Pros and Cons for Real Estate … https://andersonadvisors.com/biggerpockets-review/

What Is a Turnkey Property? How It's Used as an Investment https://www.investopedia.com/terms/t/turnkey-property.asp

The Benefits of Investing in Turnkey Rental Homes https://ohiocashflow.com/the-benefits-of-investing-in-turnkey-rental-homes/

Debunking the 7 Myths and Misconceptions About Turnkey … https://www.biggerpockets.com/blog/myths-of-turnkey-investing

How to Find the Right Turnkey Real Estate Investment Company https://smartlandturnkey.com/blog/how-to-find-the-right-turnkey-real-estate-investment-company-for-you/

Real Estate Investment Loans: Pros and Cons - RCN Capital https://rcncapital.com/blog/real-estate-investment-loans-pros-and-cons

11 Creative Financing Strategies for Real Estate Investing https://www.landlordstudio.com/blog/creative-financing-real-estate

The Ultimate Guide to Leverage in Real Estate Investment https://expresscapitalfinancing.com/blog/the-ultimate-guide-to-leverage-in-real-estate-investment-2/

How To Get the Best Mortgage Rate https://www.bankrate.com/mortgages/how-to-get-the-best-mortgage-rate/

How to do a real estate market analysis like a pro https://learn.roofstock.com/blog/real-estate-market-analysis

10 useful tech tools for savvy real estate investors https://www.stessa.com/blog/tech-tools-for-real-estate-investors/

The Importance of Location in Real Estate Development https://primior.com/importance-of-location-in-real-estate-development/

Library of Real Estate Case Studies https://www.adventuresincre.com/real-estate-case-studies/

10 Common Homebuying Red Flags https://www.sofi.com/learn/content/home-buying-red-flags/

How to Value Real Estate Investment Property https://www.investopedia.com/articles/mortgages-real-estate/11/valuing-real-estate.asp

The Due Diligence Checklist for Turnkey Real Estate ... https://blog.reination.com/the-due-diligence-checklist-for-turnkey-real-estate-investors

How to Read and Decipher Your Home Inspection Report https://www.angi.com/articles/how-read-home-inspection-report.htm

The 7 Best Tenant Screening Services of 2024 https://www.investopedia.com/best-tenant-screening-services-5070361

Guidance on Application of the Fair Housing Act to the ... - HUD https://www.hud.gov/sites/dfiles/FHEO/documents/FHEO_Guidance_on_Screening_of_Applicants_for_Rental_Housing.pdf

10 Benefits of Hiring a Property Manager | APM https://www.allpropertymanagement.com/resources/hiring-a-property-manager/10-reasons-to-hire-a-property-manager/

The Landlord's Preventative Property Maintenance Checklist https://www.avail.co/education/guides/complete-guide-to-rental-property-maintenance/preventative-maintenance-checklist

The Top 5 Practices for Ethical Investing in Real Estate https://equity.report/the-top-5-practices-for-ethical-investing-in-real-estate/

How to Build a Positive Landlord-Tenant Relationship https://drk-realty.com/commercial-real-estate-news-articles/how-to-build-a-positive-landlord-tenant-relationship

Best Practices to Build Long-Term Relationships with Real ... https://easyreadernews.com/best-practices-to-build-long-term-relationships-with-real-estate-clients/

The Crucial Role of Community Impact in Real Estate https://www.larealtors.org/blog/the-crucial-role-of-community-impact-in-real-estate-why-realtors-make-a-difference

10 Risks of Real Estate Investing to Know Before You Buy https://www.azibo.com/blog/risks-of-real-estate-investing

Real Estate Investing: Assessing Risks and Maximizing ... https://gallaghermohan.com/blogs/real-estate-investing-assessing-risks-and-maximizing-returns/

Real Estate Portfolio Diversification https://www.1031crowdfunding.com/diversifying-your-real-estate-investment-portfolio/

10 Types of Insurance for Real Estate Investors to Consider https://www.obieinsurance.com/blog/insurance-for-real-estate-investors

The best real estate podcasts for agents and brokers in 2024 https://www.housingwire.com/articles/best-real-estate-podcasts/

Top 10 Real Estate Forums for Real Estate Investors And ... https://www.landlordstudio.com/blog/real-estate-forums

10 Books All Real Estate Investors Should Read https://www.kiavi.com/blog/best-books-on-real-estate-investing

Top 11 Real Estate Events 2023 That You Can't Miss https://therealestatetrainer.com/top-real-estate-events-you-can't-miss/

Selling A Rental Property: A Complete Guide https://www.quickenloans.com/learn/selling-a-rental-property

Sell Your Rental Property: 6 Reasons Why It's Time https://www.evernest.co/blog/sell-your-rental-property-6-reasons-why-its-time

How to Refinance Your Investment Property https://www.investopedia.com/how-to-refinance-your-investment-property-5197460

10 Real Estate Investing Strategies for Long-Term Wealth https://bontefilipidis.com/10-real-estate-investing-strategies-for-long-term-wealth/

6 Insanely Inspiring Real Estate Investing Success Stories https://learn.roofstock.com/blog/real-estate-investing-success-stories

7-Step Antidote to Cure Analysis Paralysis | Real Estate Blog https://www.biggerpockets.com/blog/cure-analysis-paralysis

John Jensen | Experts https://www.colliers.com/en/experts/john-jensen

Landlords and Tenants: Tips on Avoiding Disputes https://www.marylandattorneygeneral.gov/Pages/CPD/landlords.aspx

Accredited Investor: Duties and Requirements https://www.investopedia.com/terms/a/accreditedinvestor.asp

www.ingramcontent.com/pod-product-compliance
Lightning Source LLC
Chambersburg PA
CBHW060928140726
47996CB00001B/421